The Sea Chest

By

June A Sharp

Copyright © 2025 June A Sharp

ISBN: 978-1-917778-77-0

All rights reserved, including the right to reproduce this book, or portions thereof in any form. No part of this text may be reproduced, transmitted, downloaded, decompiled, reverse engineered, or stored, in any form or introduced into any information storage and retrieval system, in any form or by any means, whether electronic or mechanical without the express written permission of the author.

This is a work of fiction. Names and characters are the product of the author's imagination and any resemblance to actual persons, living or dead, is entirely coincidental.

The views expressed in this work are solely those of the author and do not necessarily reflect the views of the publisher, and the publisher hereby disclaims any responsibility for them.

CHAPTER 1

Jane met her husband Michael when she was eighteen and he was nineteen, at the end of the Great War. They both lived in the village of Uphall, near Edinburgh and he was finishing a university course in the city, which would give him qualifications to allow him to become a manager in the new industry of shale oil extraction which was taking place locally.

Their wedding was a year later and his graduation the same year, so they took up residence in a house near to where he would work. It was little more than an oil worker's cottage in the middle of the village but Jane took great pride in scrubbing and cleaning it, so that it was the finest in the row. All her young life had been spent helping her mother to clean, bake and garden so she would become a perfect wife and she used the skills learnt in this apprenticeship to enrich the life of her new, beloved husband.

Michael had previously thought only of his studies and now they had come to an end he imagined putting the same energies into his work. To have married a good housekeeper was, for him, yet another feather in his cap and one of which he had not been totally ignorant when he pursued this attractive girl. There was no chance he would have married without researching his future bride as fully as he would study a new mining operation.

So both were truly happy in that they had achieved their own personal goals. Each morning when he took up his new employment, he would kiss his wife goodbye, never enquiring what she intended to do that day, nor did he appear to care. It was a disappointment to him that the shale oil mines were gradually closing down, so that by the time he started work he was involved in processing oil from the Persian Gulf because the Uphall mine had closed down. Having studied the history and methods of extraction from shale-rich rock since before the end of the Great War, he hoped that he could put his knowledge into practice when peacetime became the norm. Unfortunately, most of this knowledge was now defunct; but if there was one thing Michael loved it was learning something new, so he immersed himself in his books, night after night, leaving Jane without conversation. She spent her time knitting or crocheting and tried not to worry about her silent life. After all, he was trying to improve their life-style.

"Goodbye, Jane," he said perfunctorily one morning and, picking up his briefcase, left the cottage.

"Goodbye," Jane muttered to the closed door, as she watched him striding off past the window, with never a backward glance. He had stopped kissing her goodbye. Was this really all there was to marriage? Other married girls seemed so cheerful when she met them in the street and yet she found it hard to be happy with her own lot. Her mother had told her all about the 'birds and the bees' when she had become engaged, so there was no surprise when Michael took her in his arms on their wedding night. His lovemaking had been gentle and loving and Jane could hardly wait for the next time. But sadly, there were very few next times. Almost every night they went to bed, she was given a rapid kiss on the cheek and Michael turned onto his side and began to snore. Only one or two occasions saw them close together in each others arms, doing what young married couples did on a regular basis.

Four months later, however, Jane went to see the kind old doctor who had brought her into the world and he confirmed that she was pregnant. She thanked God she was normal and raced home to make a special meal for Michael to celebrate their good fortune. After what seemed like hours of waiting, she heard the door handle turn and rushed the length of the room, as he entered.

"Michael, I have something to tell you", she gushed, her face covered in one big smile.

"Let me get into the house first," he mumbled and Jane knew he had had a difficult day.

"Alright, my love," she said, helping him off with his coat and going to take hold of his briefcase.

"And I'll thank you for leaving that document case alone," he said sharply.

"I - I'm sorry. I was just so excited, I thought it would speed things up."

"Do I have to be rushed around as soon as I enter my own home? What is it this time? Did you make an apple pie or was it a Victoria sponge which has made you so excited. You're behaving like a wee girl!"

Jane's defences came down all around her and she turned her back on the ill-tempered man in an attempt to recover her equilibrium. Suddenly, she felt herself spinning round and she was hurled into an armchair at the far side of the room. Michael was looking at her with hate in his eyes and he said,

"Don't ever come to the door in that childish fashion again. Do you hear me! Never!"

She felt no disappointment. She felt no fear. All she felt was loathing. This man was her husband and she had wanted him to take pleasure in the fact that he was about to become a father. Now she would keep her secret for as long as she wished.

"Don't worry about that," she said quietly and got up from her prone position and walked to the kitchen area. There were less than five strides across the room in either direction but even these were too much for her traumatised body and she wobbled, knocking her hip on the table.

"Been at the gin, have you?" laughed Michael and she fought to control the anger which exhorted her to turn and slap his face; rubbing the sore place on her leg instead she kept her eyes averted and continued in her passage to the oven. Amazingly, he made no comment.

000

There were so many new people in the village left from the boom in oil and the quiet little street was turned into a busy thoroughfare, now the men had returned from war. It was strange to hear women with strong Irish accents ordering their groceries but these were the wives of the hard-working navvies who had constructed railways and mine shafts before the shale started to diminish. Every day, Jane was given a run-down of operations from one shopkeeper or another and it was clear that the mines in Uphall were still closing down, even though this small place had been called the oil capital of the world for a decade. The remaining four or five oil companies had amalgamated to form Scottish Oils and, although their headquarters were in Glasgow, the Technical Department was at Middleton Hall at the east end of the village and many new houses had been built to accommodate new employees. All this information had been gleaned from shop owners or customers because Michael never told her anything about his work. Had she presumed to start a conversation regarding such a masculine topic, Jane knew she would be shouted down and more or less told to get back to women's work.

CHAPTER 2

Jane hugged her secret as a child hugs its teddy bear. She could feel the baby growing inside her and vowed to take good care of herself so that he or she had the best possible start in life. Her shopping trips in the village became exercise for her and the new tiny body and she held herself erect and fought back the temptation to stick out her stomach in advertisement of her condition. The result of all this was that she remained slim and did not look pregnant for weeks longer than was normal. Michael didn't notice any difference, even in the few times he satisfied himself in bed.

In her fifth month she decided to inform Michael. Her hormones had changed her from an independent, secretive person into a loving and easy-going, feminine individual. Why should she hide the fact of her pregnancy from the one person who would benefit from it? She felt guilty for concealing it for so long. Saturday morning was the ideal time. They had slept late and Jane crept out of bed first, so she could prepare a proper cooked breakfast. She fried some bacon she had bought on one of her outings and trimmed the previous evening, and then added some of Michael's favourite, black pudding, and held back the eggs until they were both ready to eat.

"Where's my clean shirt?" came a shout from above.

"Hanging near the boiler to air!" she called back.

Silence.

In about five minutes, he appeared, dressed smartly. Jane had no idea he was going anywhere special but no doubt she would find out. She cooked the eggs and placed a plate full of breakfast on each side of the table. Knowing how Michael liked her to remain silent at meals, she began to eat slowly, looking up at him occasionally to check whether the food was to his liking. He continued to eat seriously, keeping his eyes on the plate until it was clean.

She judged the time to be right and opened her mouth to speak but before she could issue forth a syllable, Michael said,

"I'm playing golf this morning and intend to join the club. Saturday is the day when some of my colleagues at work play" and without another word he got up from the table and walked to the door.

"I found out I'm expecting a baby," she said, calmly and quietly.

"Good. I wondered if there was something wrong with you. I'll be out for lunch and see you later."

That was it.

000

The days passed pleasantly. Jane worked in the house or the garden in the mornings and sometimes went to the village shops. In the afternoons she tried to rest with a book but found that she read about half a page and then fell asleep. In the evenings, Michael came home for his meal and closeted himself with his books afterwards, until bedtime. Conversation was at a minimum and saved for necessities. Affection was non-existent.

One day Jane felt a pain in her abdomen and thought she must have eaten something which didn't agree with her. Since she became pregnant, her likes and dislikes had changed considerably. But fifteen minutes later, there was another, much more obvious pain and she wondered whether she was having contractions, as the doctor had explained would happen. It was much too early and she chose to ignore the feelings, until more and closer together pains came along, so she knew it was her time. She knocked on the adjoining wall, knowing her neighbour would be sitting at her table or at her fireside and Mrs Mullen came dashing round, saying,

"What's wrong hen, is it the babby coming? I thought you telt me you had another three or four weeks."

"That's what I did think but my contractions seem to be coming every ten minutes now."

"Och, dinnae fach yoursel. I'll go for the wifey doon the road."

Jane knew the midwife was very local, so she just sat quietly until the two women reappeared. When they entered the room she stood up and felt a trickle of liquid running down her thighs.

"That's it dearie. Your waters have broken. It won't be long now. Go and put the kettle on Jessie. We'll be needing some hot water very soon."

So the kind-hearted Mrs Wilson rushed off to the tap and put the gas on.

CHAPTER 3

Michael arrived home to find his wife in bed and a baby boy in a crib by her side. She had expected him to pay no attention to the tiny mite and to disappear into his closed room as before but his reaction to the child was one she had not anticipated. Of course, no comment was made to her, nor did he ask any questions about the birth itself or who had helped her at the time but the minute he knew it was a boy his face was wreathed in smiles. Jane could swear she saw tears run down his cheeks as he bent down and scooped up his son and his expression was that of true devotion. Perhaps this is what was needed to make him feel like a family man. Perhaps their life would take on new meaning.

"My boy, my boy!" he said, as he held the bundle of blankets close to his chest. "Henry Michael Donaldson, welcome to the world." The deed was done. He had a name, immediately and without discussion. Then the baby began to cry and the bundle was ceremoniously handed over to Jane, without a word.

000

As Henry grew, so did Michael's love for him. There were no more late nights at work. He wished to know everything the baby had done during the day and gave Jane detailed instructions as to the way he should spend his time. He was a changed man. He started to pay more attention to the house and the way the furniture was arranged and would often move chairs around or change the position of a sideboard or a chest of drawers. From being a man who cared nothing for his home surroundings, he became minutely aware of everything in a room. Books were aligned perfectly and set on a shelf so that they graded down in height; curtains were straightened when he entered the house; dust was wiped away from skirting boards. Indeed, sometimes Jane worried for his sanity.

One evening he turned the key in the lock and entered the house breezily. Henry was just over a year old and was already in bed but Michael walked through to his cot and bent to kiss his sleeping face. The child awoke. Without a word, Michael picked him out of the cot and sat him on his knee. Of course Henry was delighted but Jane had half-prepared a meal and was annoyed that it would be disturbed by a child who had already run rings around her for the whole day.

"Couldn't you leave him in his cot?" she said in exasperation, as she banged the pots about on the stove. She drained the potatoes noisily, added butter and a drop of milk, then cast around for her potato masher. At least she could make the shepherd's pie and heat it up in the oven if necessary.

Michael put the child down and she thought this was something unusual. He was actually doing as she asked. She looked up from the steaming potatoes and smiled, then saw him marching furiously towards her and she was scared. He took her chin between his thumb and forefinger, and she thought he was going to kiss her, so she pursed her lips in readiness. But then he took her other hand with his free hand and plunged it straight into the pan of steaming potatoes.

Her mind went numb. The pain was excruciating and he still had hold of her face, even though her tears were now pouring onto his fingers. At last he let go and she thrust her white-encrusted hand onto his head. She wanted to hurt him but she was in too much pain to do anything more. Remembering what her mother had told her about scalds, she looked around feverishly and found the washing up bowl full of dirty cold water, where she plunged her poor hand, causing the liquid to go cloudy and her hand to appear bright red. Old tea-leaves and uneaten biscuits rose to the surface but she moved her hand around in it slowly, feeling the pain dissipating. All this time, Michael had been clutching her lower jaw in his vice-like grip, even while she was splashing around in the bowl. She noticed his hair covered in mashed potato and part of her felt like laughing but she knew this must be hysteria because nothing was remotely funny. Then, he released her and she started to run the cold tap into the muddy water. All her thoughts were for her own pain; there were none to spare for anyone or anything else.

"Perhaps you will think twice before you tell me what to do, woman!" he spat into her face, before turning around and gently picking up the little boy, who had been holding the side of his cot and watching the performance in amazement. Michael kissed him on the forehead and took hold of one of his chubby, little hands, with the hand which had previously pressed into his mother's cheeks. The child relaxed into his father's love, thinking that all must be well because daddy was smiling at him.

000.

CHAPTER 4

Jane's hand recovered, although her skin bore the results of the hot potato mixture for months. Her mind bore the results also.

A depression had started in England and spread to Scotland, where it had become worse. Jane worried that Michael would find himself out of a job, due to the way he continued to treat people. If a man was below him in status, he demeaned him considerably both in private and in public but should anyone hold a senior position or a title, he almost fell over his feet to abase himself. There were many in Scottish Oils who would take pleasure in removing him from office. However, his deferential manner appeared to charm his superiors because, as men were losing their jobs, Michael hung on grimly.

The wife of one of Michael's colleagues at work was pregnant, so it was decided that Jane would have another baby. And Andrew was born in February 1924. Jane longed for the warmer weather, when she could divest him of his thick layer of shawls and blankets.

CHAPTER 5

At the end of April she had a nasty scare, when she developed a cough and a high temperature. Her neighbour ran for the doctor and Jane spent her time in bed worrying about Henry and the baby while she lay sweating. Influenza had killed 800 people since the beginning of the year and she was terrified that her boys would be deprived of a mother at the beginning of their lives. This had the effect of raising her temperature even more and the sombre expression of Dr Hargreaves as he administered to her made her certain that she would succumb. He promised to return the following day and her neighbour, Mrs Mullen, said she would tend to the children. When Michael came back from work, the first thing he did was to send her away, saying he would do whatever was necessary.

"How can you look after two babies alone, Michael", Jane asked while her head pounded and her eyes began to close.

"Easily," he said. "I don't know why women make such a fuss about caring for children."

The thought of his feeding them, changing their nappies and putting them to bed filled Jane with horror. She was so glad she had put Andrew onto a bottle. She could vaguely hear the clattering of cutlery and the gurgling of the children, just before she drifted into a long sleep induced by the doctor's medicine.

Next morning she awoke when the light filtered through a gap in the curtains and she was surprised to find herself much recovered. The noises she had heard the previous evening were being repeated and only stopped when there was a knock at the front door.

"Oh, hello Mrs Mullen, you're just in time," she heard Michael say. "I must go off to work now and I will leave these two angels in your capable hands."

Her neighbour said a few sentences in reply and the front door slammed in its usual fashion, before Mrs Mullen's head appeared around the door of her room.

"I hope my husband managed last night. You see I fell asleep and knew nothing until about half an hour ago," Jane said, hoisting herself up in the warm bed.

"Oh, you can rest assured my dear, everything is totally ship-shape down there. But then I suppose he told you all that before he left. What a good husband you've got yourself. Those babies are washed, dressed and fed and he looked quite the thing, going off to work all spick and span, as if nothing was any the different. Now, my love, how are you feeling, yourself?"

Jane's high temperature had gone and she had not woken herself during the night by coughing. In fact she wondered if it had all been a bad dream.

"I seem to be better, Mrs Mullen," she grinned, as she thought of all that the woman had said about Michael and the children. He certainly knew how to fabricate. He was an out and out liar. Thank goodness he had looked after the children properly but then he would, wouldn't he, just to prove how easy it was.

"Well, you can just stay there, hen, until the doctor comes. He left you in my care and I don't intend to let him down. I expect you've had some breakfast and a drink, have you?"

"No, not a thing since you left yesterday."

"That's unbelievable but you said you've been asleep, so I can't blame your dear husband. Anyway, I'll bring you something nice and light and we'll see how you feel after that."

Off she went into the kitchen and Jane could hear her cooing to the boys as she went. There was no point in trying to explain how Michael behaved towards her because nobody would believe it. He was an actor and had learned his lines extremely well.

Dr Hargreaves arrived in the middle of the morning, to find the house completely tidy, Henry in his playpen with his toys, Andrew asleep in his pram and Jane propped up on her pillows, reading. Mrs Mullen was flicking a duster around and moving ornaments about to prove to the doctor that she had done his bidding. The only thing she omitted to tell him was that Michael had thrown her out the previous day and done everything himself.

"Right, Jane. Let me take a look in your mouth," he said, in his officious way. "Say ah! Oh yes, just as I thought. Nothing much to be seen. Now, I'm going to listen to your chest. I don't have to tell you how to do this, do I? You've done it all many times before," he said, totally forgetting how few times she had seen him as a child. Her health had been the envy of many of her mother's friends. "That's good," said the doctor, as he wound up his stethoscope and put it away in his bag. "Perfectly normal, my dear. Now, I must tell you what I thought of all your high jinks yesterday. I know you imagined you had this dreadful influenza which is catching people out all over the British Isles but you must remember you lead such a healthy life up here in God's Own Country and the ones who are coming down with the 'flu are the people who maunder about in the smog and smoke of the cities. What you had yesterday was a little spot of exhaustion, brought on by looking after your bairns and the way you knock yourself out to keep this little place like a palace. The best advice I can give you is to take life easy for a while – not that it will do much good, I know. At least try to grab half-an-hour when your weans are asleep, to read or sew or do something sedentary. There! I've done my bit. Now it's your turn" and with a flourish and a goodbye to Mrs Mullen, he picked up his bag and left.

Jane could not believe she had been stricken down by exhaustion. She kept herself fit and well and was constantly on the go. To take life easy was not part of her nature but she must do as the doctor ordered, somehow. Maybe now it was spring, she would be able to relax a little more, as long as Michael had no more ideas about expanding his family.

CHAPTER 6

More sunny days brought more growth in the tiny garden and Jane found she enjoyed nothing better than spreading a rug on the grass and taking her two children outside to play, while she poked around in the neglected flower beds. Henry sat engrossed in his own small world which consisted of wooden blocks and soft toys. He was a quiet, calm child compared with Andrew, who never sat still for a minute. To Andrew the whole of life was a challenge and he had cried and yelled his way through babyhood, demanding attention most of the time he was awake. Even now, Andrew would call his mother away from her ministrations just to see what he had found in the earth. More often than not, it was a worm he had dug up and one of his favourite occupations was finding a new home for his finds.

"Mamma, I put the worm in flower," he would say and Jane had to explain that worms did not enjoy being up in the air but needed to burrow in the earth. So the rest of that day would be spent making holes in which to nestle whole families of earthworms.

The garden became Jane's comfort and solace. No matter how much Michael shouted at her and whatever the behaviour of the boys, she would look forward to her digging and planting, when they finally settled down. It was a small patch which had once been planted out by one of the local miners but had been left to grow into a conglomeration of weeds. She wondered what he would have thought of all this neglect of his pride and joy; for miners always seemed to want to wallow in nature when they returned from underground; something she understood, for who would want to spend their working life in the dark with only a lamp to guide him and no colour to be seen. What a desperate way to live.

When she first stood at her back door and surveyed the scene of her weedy patch, it should have been a daunting prospect but, to Jane it was just one more challenge. When she first borrowed Mrs Mullen's old mower to make a space for her tartan rug, she felt like a white hunter scything her way through the jungle; in fact half the job was done with her kitchen scissors. And, once the masses of cow parsley and tall grass had been removed, it was a case of forking over the ground. Her father had gone on about double-digging but one of his friends had whispered to her that it was not really necessary, so she chose to work on those principles and only dug out the old roots. That accomplished, she felt an overpowering sense of achievement, and working on the overgrown borders a foot at a time was easy. At least the size of the plot meant that she was never far away from her children, her responsibilities, her only love. She knew that most mothers would guard their offspring from the dirt and danger of the garden but she saw it as a way they could learn to grow up naturally, in the confines of their own great outdoors and she could teach them all they needed to know about safety whilst they dug and muddied themselves.

For a time, Michael would come home from his laboratory and find her still absorbed in her attempts to encourage small cuttings to grow. These were begged from the owners of gardens she passed on her route to the village shops and planted in old pots she had found hidden at the bottom of the garden. He had a negative way of looking at life and would constantly shrug his shoulders and say,

"Why do you want to be bothered with those silly little bits of grass. You'll never get them to grow. It's just a waste of time."

What he did not realise was that this made her all the more determined to make them survive and she hid them away in corners and usually ensured that she had washed away most of her own grime before he appeared. Her attempts to interest herself in his pursuits were still put to ridicule but she continued to enquire about his achievements at work. She knew that chemists were the foundation of the oil industry because they were capable of streamlining the operations carried out to move the now necessary crude oil from one place to another in the least costly manner. With a financial depression spreading from county to county in Britain, this was imperative, in order to save the whole industry from annihilation.

A brief question like, "How did you get on today?" was greeted with grumbling comments, such as,

"What do you care? It has nothing to do with children or bits of plants, so I don't know why you ask."

But she continued to enquire, sometimes just to hear the pessimistic retorts and to comfort herself with the thought that she could never behave in this way. She was gratified by his attention to the children because his attitude would help to form their perspective of life, long after they grew up and had left their parents and after he had gone.

She wrote her thoughts in her journal in quiet moments when the boys were sleeping or playing contentedly and this reflection, after he had gone, would flit into her mind and then disappear as quickly as it had arrived. It had a consoling ring to it, almost a soothing thought when things had been particularly difficult between them. This was probably how infamous murders had been done in the past. The thought of not having to experience any more sadistic, mentally cruel comments hung around like a bride's bouquet thrown from the carriage as she left the assembled crowd. But it never dropped. No-one caught it and became the next lucky girl. Ideas ran through Jane's mind, as she planted and watered her seedlings. Luckily, due to the presence of children, there was not a chance in the world that she would plant such items as digitalis, laburnum trees, belladonna, monkshood and many others, which she knew from her avid reading were poisonous. They would hardly be detected in a glass of whisky.

She thrust these thoughts from her mind, whenever they entered it. What was she thinking? She was starting to have the ideas of a villain.

CHAPTER 7

Back in the journal a few years later, the day Michael came home and said they were moving house, Jane was unsure of her feelings She was happy enough in the village where she had lived all her life, although it was feeling a little cramped in the cottage, now that the boys had been at school for a while. They shared a bedroom in the attic and seemed to be quite happy doing so, sitting around the table together in the living room to play games. If Michael wanted some peace, he would retreat to their bedroom. Then one day, he looked up and said,

"I've been promoted to Manager and I feel we can afford a bigger house, to reflect my status. I've had people looking around for me and one of my men has come up with a detached house in Ecclesmachan, not far away. It seems to be going at the price I had in mind, so I thought we should take it. My lawyer is drawing up the papers as we speak. Obviously, I've had a look at it and I'm sure it will be suitable. All you have to do is organise the decoration and the curtains, of course."

So, it was a fait accompli and all Jane had to do was the hard work, of course.

The following day, after finding out the address, Jane walked down the lane, which led from the corner in Uphall opposite the inn. As she turned onto the Ecclesmachan Road, she passed Robertson's grocery shop and made a mental note to pick up some flour on her way home. There were children sitting on the pavement-edge playing marbles in the gutter, who waved to her as she walked on. Their bare knees were filthy and one little boy picked his dirty nose, calmly inspecting his trophy before putting it in his mouth. Did Henry and Andrew do this when they went out to play with their friends?

It had been a warm April and she remembered reading yesterday in the newspaper that the weather in London had been the hottest for fifty years; but Scottish weather was always a bit cooler. However, it was no wonder that she felt the need to remove her thick cardigan, as she ploughed on down the country lane towards the church of St Nicholas. Another article in the paper had been about a new divorce bill which had been passed by Parliament and was intended to make it easier for women in unhappy marriages to divorce their husbands, without having to leave home first. She had yet to see her new home, let alone plan to leave it but the piece in the newspaper had drawn it to her attention that women could and did obtain divorces from men who treated them badly. Obviously, these were women who had private incomes, not poor souls like herself who needed the man's income to keep body and soul together – and make sure her children were fed and clothed.

Her walk had become something of a trial, with the unusual heat of the day and the increased number of motorcars chugging past her and surrounding her with fumes from their exhaust pipes. Some had their hoods down and Jane noticed that many were driven by women, wearing large floppy hats or hair-bands over their short tresses. These innovations had come with peacetime, as women claimed their rightful, independent places in society but she had not expected to find such modern behaviour in the backwoods of rural Scotland. They must be visitors from Edinburgh or Glasgow.

She passed the high stone walls of the churchyard and continued to march on towards the next tiny village, named Ecclesmachan, a corruption of the French description, 'eglise de St Machan', because it housed the church of that name. Now, Jane's interest was only in the line of stone-built houses ahead. She loved this slightly grey sandstone, seeing it as a mark of strength and she stood for some minutes ogling the size of the pieces of stone used to build the detached building standing in its formal garden in front of her. It must have taken two or three men to carry each stone, as they gradually formed a house in the last century. She wandered round the house and peeked through a piece of broken fence into the large garden and was delighted with the outside only, and that was very important to her.

So she had seen it and it passed her inspection. Living here in such a palatial manner would be so different from being a cottage dweller in Uphall but she would be able to keep up with her acquaintances in the village, by shopping as she always did every two or three days. At school time in the morning and afternoon, the boys could catch the SMT bus, which rolled along on its rigid wheels, hail or shine. Michael would back his Austin out of the drive and along the country lane, as she had seen the sophisticated ladies doing earlier and all would be well. At least all would seem to be well and she would not be the one to upset their particular apple-cart – not yet.

When she reached the junction with the Glasgow to Edinburgh Road, passing the tailor's shop and giving him a friendly wave, she remembered her need for flour from the grocer. She knew it came from Houstoun Mill just down the road, where the local farmers took their corn to be worked into flour and on many occasions in the past she had watched the complicated process after school, with the son of the miller, Alex Hastings, who lived with his parents at Braehead Cottage on the road which went up to the home farm for the big house. She had been fascinated by the way the water from the burn turned the huge wheel, which in turn rotated millstones to grind the grain. This, combined with watching the dirty-faced shale workers coming off shift, had been childhood entertainment, albeit humble, for Jane and her friends.

The grocer stood in the doorway, wearing his long green apron and moved deferentially aside as she entered.

"What can I do for you, this fine day?" he said in his musical Glaswegian voice.

"A bag of flour, if you please, Mr Robertson," she replied and foraged in her pocket for her purse. While she was thus occupied, the door opened and a stranger came in, wearing a shirt with sleeves rolled up past his elbows. And he was dangling the ubiquitous tweed jacket from his forefinger, at his shoulder. Jane noticed what fine, muscular forearms he had and how deeply coloured they were. Although his hair was mousey, the hair on his arms was fair due to the bleaching action of the sun. He must be a farm worker but it was unusual to see one with a tweed jacket, mid-week.

"Hello, Rob!" Mr Robertson said.

"Hello yourself, Ewan. It's a fine day."

"Aye, a fine day for a dip in the burn if you ask me. Even though it's only April, it's certainly too hot to be indoors but beggars can't be choosers."

"I like that. Call yourself a beggar do you? I've never seen a richer beggar!"

The two continued their good-natured banter until the grocer remembered he was in the throes of measuring out a bag of flour for Jane and looked back at her apologetically.

"I expect you two know each other, don't you?"

Both shook their heads and stared at each other.

"Well, this is Mrs Donaldson from down the road, Rob, and this rude fellow is Mr Robert Barclay, who's working on the garden at the big house. They both said how do you do and smiled as they shook hands. Jane had never felt such a warm grasp and such firm, dry hands. Was it her imagination that he hung onto her hand for just a little longer than was necessary? She was daydreaming again, not having had even a touch of hands from her husband.

She took out the coins and paid for her purchase, saying thanks to the grocer as she left the shop and stepped out into the warm afternoon sun. Because she was never offered any affection from her husband, thoughts of a flirtatious nature tended to assail her when she was confronted by any man who was vaguely attractive. She must clear her silly mind and stop thinking like a teenager, then hurry if she were to get home before the boys came back from school, and put her flour to good use in the pie she had planned for tea. So, off she strode towards the cottage she would soon be leaving forever and thoughts circled about her mind regarding the new residence they would soon inhabit.

She had noticed the large house had been empty, which meant that they would be able to move as soon as missives had been signed, presuming their offer was accepted. She could not see Michael putting in an offer unless he was sure he would succeed.

CHAPTER 8

The house became theirs the following week and plans were put into action to move them out of the friendly little cottage and into the mausoleum which had been inhabited by an old lady, who had lived alone until her death at the end of last year. Jane felt it was right to begin a new life in the spring, just as the trees and garden plants did, and she started looking forward to working in her much larger garden when the weather began to improve in earnest. The boys were overjoyed to be going to a house where they could go upstairs to bed, each in his own room – a thing which was unheard-of in the cottage fraternity. Jane hoped they would not mind being so far away from their friends and from their school.

The move itself was simple; the carrier appeared on the doorstep one morning, their furniture was loaded, it arrived at the new house within the hour and everything was put into place immediately. Michael made sure he was in the hall, directing operations and made his own decisions about which pieces went into which rooms. Jane could see herself transferring furniture surreptitiously for months afterwards. However, if this was all it took to make him reasonably happy, she could accept it. The main thing was to avoid any arguments, particularly while they were moving in and the boys were around.

To expect his new house to magically fabricate a new character for Michael was like expecting a wasp to stop stinging once it was established in a new nest. Their first night at Ecclesmachan should have been a memory to treasure for life. Jane felt light-headed and wandered from room to room, luxuriating in the spacious interiors. She had never imagined visiting, let alone living in, such a mansion and she felt a great surge of gratitude well up inside her towards Michael. A man who took his family to such a grand dwelling must harbour feelings of love towards them, surely; after all a man could live anywhere alone.

Jane had prepared a meal in advance, so that the removal work in progress would not be interrupted by a shout for the whereabouts of her oven or for her saucepans. She laid her big terracotta dish out on the kitchen table and called Michael and the boys. Her husband was first to arrive and she smiled at him gently.

"What's this?" he growled, looking round the room.

"I made it yesterday," she said, apologetically, imagining his disapproval was for a meal which was less than fresh.

"I don't care when you made it, girl. I'm sure it will be edible. It's just that I seem to remember that we have moved into a proper house now, which has a dining room. There will be no more bothy meals such as farmhands eat in this house!"

Jane could hardly believe her ears. It was the first evening in a new house and she had taken the trouble to ensure that her family would be fed and her crazy husband wanted his meal in a dining room, which had as much furniture inside it as a rabbit hutch. Andrew and Henry bustled in at that very moment, pushing each other around and laughing into each others' faces, so she redirected her attention to her sons and asked them to wash their hands before coming to the table.

"Did you hear me?" Michael said, thrusting his face into hers.

"Yes, I did," Jane replied quietly "and I chose to ignore it. Apart from anything else, we don't have a table in the dining room; unless you intended us to move the kitchen table in there."

"Don't you..."

"Here come the boys. At least let them enjoy their first meal in the new house."

Amazingly, he refrained from further comment and the repast was completed without any more shouting. The mess was cleared away, the boys were settled into their separate rooms and Jane staggered back into the sitting room. It had been a most exhausting day.

Then later the sarcasm and insulting criticisms began. Michael's voice permeated the large room, bouncing around the naked walls. Had there been curtains at the windows, they might have soaked up some of the vitriolic bawling but, as it was, the only sponge in the room was Jane and she had reached saturation point. The only way she knew of tolerating such a tirade of abuse was to ignore it, to send her thoughts away to pastures green, and the place she chose was a hill outside Uphall. She had walked around her village, saying goodbye to her childhood haunts and found herself in farming country beyond the old cemetery. The farm track wound its way up and up, until there was nothing except a small copse, with a couple of felled trees in front. She had sat down on a log and looked across wide fields to the Pentland Hills and this had given her the peace and strength to go ahead with the house move. Now, she used the memory of it to extricate herself from this sordid scene. Nothing could hurt her as long as she had her own memories.

Michael knew she had switched off her attention and it had the effect of stopping him in his tracks. To shout and yell at no-one was no pleasure and she had become a non-person in his eyes.

He was a blatant attention-seeker, just like a child when its mother is immersed in a newspaper or a book. Jane remembered Andrew putting his tiny fist through the newsprint many times when he had wanted her to watch him playing and Henry had been the same; the only difference was that Henry had grown out of it.

"I'm going to bed, Michael," she said woodenly and walked away, knowing that she must sleep in the same room as him. Would it be possible for them to use separate rooms now? This was not the time to mention it but maybe sometime.

She was fearful that the noise had disturbed the children, so looked closely at both boys as she straightened their sheets and blankets. Both of them appeared to be fast asleep, Henry on his back and Andrew with his face thrust into the pillow. That was a relief. On entering her own new, vast bedroom with its few pieces of furniture dotted around the walls, she felt pleasure quickly superceded by depression. What a delight it would have been to enter this room with a man she truly loved. And to clasp each other passionately, discussing how they would make this house their own. To lie awake wondering whether Michael would want to hold her or would merely roll onto his side was a form of torture. This hit and miss relationship was not what she had visualized.

Later, her husband appeared in the bedroom and switched on the overhead light. The naked bulb glared around the room, enabling him to see what he was doing, as he sat down clumsily on the side of the bed to remove his pants and socks. Jane remained as still as she could, so that he would imagine her asleep, although it was not humanly possible for anyone to remain so in the tumult which had preceded Michael's getting in. He groaned and grumbled about the temperature of the bed, heaved the sheet and blankets around him leaving Jane without any, then placed his cold feet onto her warm legs. Thundering around and taking even more of the bedclothes away, he yawned noisily and eventually collapsed into sleep.

000

The garden had been sadly neglected, so Jane set to with a definite will to restoring it to some semblance of tidiness. She collected armfuls of old foliage from many perennial plants she did not recognise and some she knew very well. Her little cottage garden in Uphall had been crammed with everything she could beg from her neighbours, so it had been a riot of colour throughout the summer, with foxgloves, wallflowers, sweet Williams, antirrhinums, daisies of all shapes and sizes and some short-lived annuals given to her by friendly acquaintances in the local shops. The boys had loved the colourful snapdragons and had chased each other through the house, biting each other with the little 'mouths'. All these flowers had followed on from crocuses, snowdrops, daffodils and narcissus bulbs in the spring.

Now, she would have to wait for summer to see what was in this much larger garden, before she even attempted to plant anything herself. It was probably too grand for her cottage garden flowers but perhaps one or two clumps here and there would make her feel more at home. In the meantime, she must continue with the decongestion. She went down on her knees to pull out some early weeds near one of the side walls and almost fell backwards on hearing a shaky voice say, 'hello'. She looked up and saw an excessively thin woman gazing down at her through the tangled branches of a flowering currant bush. Her garden path was higher than Jane's border.

"Oh, you frightened me!" she said, without thinking and the little face took on an expression of horror.

"I am so sorry. I didn't mean to alarm you, my dear. It's just that I thought we should become acquainted, now that you have settled in." She had a high-class Edinburgh accent, with strange accentuated vowels.

"Of course, of course. What am I thinking of, saying such things." Jane stood up and brushed the dirt from her hands on her apron, making an involuntary action of straightening her hair as she looked at the old lady on the other side of the wall. Her top half was now in view and she could see a very thin, very tidy old lady of some indeterminate age. She was wearing a floral apron, with wide straps, which covered up most of her fine jumper of a pale shade of turquoise. Her hair was curled and she wore metallic spectacles on the end of her nose. Even through the glasses, Jane could see a twinkle in her blue eyes and she moved her thin, pale lipsticked lips into a sweet smile, while she proffered her hand down to Jane.

"I'm Grace Sanderson. How do you do," she said.

Jane reached up and more or less grabbed the bony, veined old hand, which was laden with diamonds, and said,

"And I'm Jane Donaldson. How do you do."

The formalities over, they both burst out laughing, Jane at the state of herself meeting her new neighbour in a welter of weeds and old foliage and Grace because she could never resist a good laugh.

"You must come in for a cup of tea and a chat. We're not very smart yet but I'm sure you won't mind, will you?"

"Of course not. It is very kind of you." She hesitated, looking directly into her face and Jane knew enough about politesse to know that she was waiting for her to firm up the invitation, so she said,

"What about tomorrow afternoon. Would that be suitable?"

"Oh yes, yes! That would be fine. I will see you then, Mrs Donaldson."

"No, just call me Jane. I will see you then, Mrs Sanderson."

The conversation was at an end and the old lady drifted away into her own garden, leaving Jane to get on with her work.

Their first meeting was just short chat and a cup of tea, when Jane got out her best china for the lovely old lady, thinking she would not be happy with mugs and mismatched plates. They discussed the local area, the shops and the buses; then Mrs Donaldson said she must be going to feed her pussy. Jane was quite happy about this, knowing that her house was anything but smart at present but making a mental note to dress up the parlour in honour of her new old friend.

CHAPTER 9

In the surprisingly warm spring weather, one Saturday, Henry and Andrew were behaving like foals when they are first introduced to new grass. Michael was nowhere to be seen, having taken an early breakfast alone and then vanished.

Weekends were sacrosanct and Jane intended to keep them that way, at least as long as the boys were at school. Now that they lived away from the village, she felt honour-bound to take them on long walks and introduce them to their new area, even though it was so close to the village of Uphall, close to where they had lived previously. Her ideas on the upbringing of children clashed with those of Michael, who felt they should entertain each other and find something practical to do with their time. So, because he was absent, she was able to call the boys down and inform them that a walk was imminent.

"Oh goodie, Mother. Where shall we go?" said Andrew, bouncing up and down at the prospect of new places.

"Will it be far?" asked Henry, more seriously.

"I thought we would do a round trip of the fields, ending up in the village, where you might see some of your school friends," Jane said and they knew her mind had been made up and no argument in the world was going to change it. So they rushed off to find boots and woollies and were standing at the front entrance when Jane appeared with her own boots and a light waterproof. She thought how middle-class they looked, walking down the gravel path with the stone house in the background and wondered what her working-class parents would have thought of this, had they been alive to see it. Reaching the gate, which led on to the road, she cautioned the boys about the dangers of carts and motorcars and turned to drop the latch. The house looked even more imposing from this angle and she immediately started to plan what colour curtains she would make and where they would require lace ones, if at all because nobody could look into their house, being at the end of the drive.

"Come on, Mother. We've a long way to go. Could I suggest we walk down past the church hall and then turn into the field on the hill?" Andrew seemed to know exactly where he was going.

"How do you know all this local geography, Andrew?" she asked.

"Only from driving to Linlithgow with Dad a couple of times. While he is intent on the motor, I spend my time looking across the fields and I know where the footpaths go now."

"Clever boy", she said and looked at Henry's dismal expression because he was not the clever boy in question. He stared down at his feet for the next half mile and then suddenly looked up, a huge smile on his face.

"I know where the farm track comes out, on the way to Binny Craig."

"Do you, smartypants?" said his younger brother. We all know what that hill's called."

"But what about the track, cleverclogs?", he replied.

"Now then, boys. Why are you fighting and where did you learn all these strange names," his mother intervened.

"At school, of course," retorted Henry "although we're not really allowed to use them. Nicknames are punished with the tawse. I haven't been given pandies yet", he said, holding out his hands. Jane knew all about that thick leather strap, wielded by many schoolmasters onto the small hands of boys, and sometimes girls. Luckily she had never had to suffer from pandies, which was what the strapping was called, probably because she was so afraid of authority that she never put a foot wrong at school. And then Henry went on rapidly to explain how he knew the route of the farm track. "You see, I met the farmer one day when he collected his little girl from school and he told me all about the fields on the way to the burn and how the track passes his farm and then twists away to Linlithgow town. What do you think of that, Andrew?"

"Very clever," smiled the younger boy and looked up conspiratorially at his mother, as if saying, I'll just humour him.

Jane was tempted to take the conversation back to the description of the tawse and when it was used in her school but she fought the temptation.

She loved to see the boys' characters forming and was glad to see that Michael's bad temper appeared to be totally missing from his offspring; otherwise, the lashings at school would be more plentiful.

They passed the church hall and schoolhouse at the end of the small village of Ecclesmachan and continued to walk at the side of the dusty and often muddy road. However, before reaching the top of the hill, there was a broken part of the fence where feet had flattened the tall grasses, brown from the hard winter.

"This is it. This is it!" shouted Andrew in his excitement at having organised his party so well.

"Over we go then, boys," Jane said and hoisted up her country skirt to climb the wooden bar. Henry held out his hand, like a true gentleman, to assist her in her clambering and Andrew rushed to climb over after her to do likewise. Like grown-up men they were fighting for the hand of the maiden, who happened in this fairy tale to be their own mother and Jane saw it as worthwhile practice for the real thing later in life.

Once off the beaten dirty track, the two young boys started to enjoy themselves, hiding behind bushes and popping out to frighten each other, seeing how far they could throw sticks found on the ground and making new paths to join up with the one on which they travelled. Jane wondered why they chose not to notice the fresh growth on the shrubs or beneath their feet and simply ignored the beautiful blue sky with its scattering of fine cloud. Perhaps this was the way of it; women looked for beauty and men for excitement.

Their walk was longer than first anticipated, so they found themselves at the end of the farm track a little out of breath and very happy to see the first houses of their old village as they rounded the corner. One of the new buses, with pneumatic tyres instead of hard wheels trundled past them on the way to Edinburgh but it was pointless even looking because Jane knew it followed the same route as its predecessor and was heading for Broxburn prior to the road into the capital city via the town of Corstorphine and not turning off where they wanted to go. With a sigh and a deep breath, Jane held out her hands to both her sons and together they swung round the garden wall of one of the new houses facing the big house of Hopetoun. As they did so, a man, who was striding down the road at the side of the large iron gates lifted his hand in greeting.

Surprised, but imagining it was someone who lived in the village and had recognised her, Jane glanced over the road and smiled but he was now crossing and she knew this friendly expression. It was Rob Barclay, the man she had met in the grocers. Hesitating, to allow him to catch up, she wished she had a hand free to smooth down her hair and check for mud splashes on her skirt but both boys held on to her hands ferociously and proprietorially.

"Hello Mrs Donaldson. It's a fine day for a walk. How far have you been today? And are these your boys? Fine-looking laddies if I might say so."

"Oh, thank you. Yes, we have been for a long walk, a round trip you might say, from Ecclesmachan, past the shale bing and down the farm track to where you see us now."

Both adults were aware of the necessity of the rubbish left behind by the shale oil industry and known locally as bings. Jane hated the sight of these piles of red rubble which messed up the countryside, blotting out much of the fine scenery. She mentally removed them from her vision and thought that, if she were a painter, she would create pictures without them, making the landscape beautiful, as it once was.

"Phew! Quite a leg-stretcher and particularly for these fellows. Do you enjoy walking, my lads, or was your mother doing it for the good of your health?!"

Then there was a gap in the conversation, while both boys stared at this strange character with an expression of amusement and curiosity. They had never met a man who spoke directly to them when an adult was present. Their own father simply ignored them when he met one of his colleagues and never included them in any conversations. Their mother did sometimes of course but women were different.

"Well! Cat got your tongues or something?" he pursued.

"N-no, sir. Mother didn't make us go. We enjoy it," Andrew said at last and Henry just grinned inanely.

"Well, you make sure she gets you a poke of sweeties from the wee shop, to help you on your way back. Where is home, anyway, Mrs Donaldson? You didn't say and neither did old Robertson when you left the shop."

"We've moved recently, to one of the houses in Ecclesmachan. It's much bigger than the cottage we had in Uphall, so there's more room for all of us now."

"Which house would that be? I do quite a bit of work in Ecclesmachan, for some of the toffs you know."

"It is Number 10, just off the main street. I think it has a name but I can't remember it – not yet."

"Then you're one of the toffs. These are great big houses for one family. I do a bit of tidying up for Mrs Sanderson on occasion. You might know her. A lovely old lady, been there for donkey's years. She used to be a friend of my mother, that is when my ma was alive. I try to keep all the big stuff in her garden a bit tidy; otherwise the old dear would start doing it herself and goodness knows what would happen then. Oh, here I go rambling on about my work again and you must want to get on with your walk."

"Not really," said Jane quietly. "We've about had enough and there's still the Ecclesmachan Road to go. We're glad of the rest, aren't we boys?"

They both nodded and then Andrew, showing more bravado, said,

"Not really. It will be fine once we get going again. Come along, troops!"

"Not so fast, Sergeant Major," said Rob. "What about a lift in my army wagon? It's nothing fancy, you understand. I use it for work all the time but I would be delighted to give you a ride home – and I can drop in on Mrs Sanderson at the same time, just to see how her garden is looking."

Jane tried to open her mouth to refuse politely but, looking down, saw Henry's tortured expression and Andrew's excited one and decided to remain silent. With the result that Rob started to walk alongside them, chatting to one boy or another as they went, and dodging out of the way of other pedestrians along the busy Saturday street to where his filthy van was parked.

He moved a trowel and fork from the front passenger seat and brushed it cursorily with one of his dirty but shapely masculine hands. Jane remembered how warm they had felt and then, hearing a noise at the back, realised that her children were being loaded like dogs, into the rear. They obviously didn't mind. The laughing and cheerful shouting was enough to make her face the front and smile, lovingly.

Rob got in, started the engine, and they chugged off down the long road home. As they rounded the bend, off the main street, Jane felt like waving in the style of the King at the people on Wallace's corner. For the first time in years, she felt like royalty, in the dirtiest vehicle that was ever cranked into activity.

As they passed the Model lodging house, Rob gave the boys a running commentary on why it had been built for travelling workers who came to the local farmers for work during the harvest or to the town authorities for road-making. For a gardener, he was very knowledgeable about many things, as Jane was to find out.

CHAPTER 10

"Would you like some Red Hot Pokers, my dear? I should have split them in the autumn but they won't come to any harm if we leave a good-sized root ball on them."

"That would be lovely, Mrs Sanderson. I have no tall plants in the front borders at all and I was wondering how to make them more colourful."

"Well, you just come along into my garden and we'll dig them up together," old Grace said, waving her trowel in the air as she spoke.

Jane had not planned to do any serious gardening when she popped outside to walk around the policies but it seemed ill-mannered to refuse such a kind offer, so she grabbed an old jacket from the hook behind the back door and walked to the end of the drive and round into Grace's garden. There was so much in there that it was hard to discern one plant from another but at least this meant that weeds had nowhere to grow. Rob would be glad of that.

She found herself thinking of him quite often since he had driven them home and stood to chat outside the gate. Grace had seen them on that occasion, from her sitting room window, and waved at them cheerfully. Unfortunately, Michael had arrived in the Austin at precisely that moment and had glowered before turning into the drive and grinding the pebbles under his wheels. The boys had been fooling around on the lawn and thought it was amusing that stones were flung into the air as their father sped towards the garage, not realising that they could easily have broken windows or given one of them a nasty bruise as he carelessly rattled along. He then got out of the car and slammed the door hard behind him and Jane had imagined that he would just stride round and enter the house, but no. He motioned to her to come forward, completely ignoring Rob and she foolishly complied, without introducing him to her husband.

"I'm sorry, Rob. It seems that Michael needs something. Thank you for your kindness and I hope to see you again, soon," she said, apologetically. Walking away, she noticed Rob staring past her at Michael and wondered how her husband could be so rude as to interrupt her conversation, without so much as a wave or hello to him. Then she realised why.

"What on Earth are you doing, talking at the front gate to a gardener? You'll have the neighbours talking about us. Don't you know that underlings are meant to be kept exactly where their name suggests – under!"

"He very kindly gave the boys and I a ride home, after a long walk. The least I could do was to thank him."

"You what! You mean to say that you allowed my sons to travel in that...that...vehicle! I can't believe this! What will you do next. Take a ride on the back of a tractor?"

"I know it isn't the smartest of motors but Henry and Andrew were tired, after our walk and ..." She got no further because Michael turned tail and walked away, calling the boys to him as if they were a pair of collies. Jane fought back the impulse to say woof-woof and followed him into the house.

000

But on this occasion, Grace's offer of plants was indeed a godsend and Jane was glad she had accepted. She desperately wanted to transform her patch of greenery into a patch of colour and, like the lady of the manor that Michael wanted her to be, she wanted her surroundings to reflect her own moods and style. Even though there would be no team of gardeners or 'underlings' to rush to collect flowers for her drawing room, she wanted to be sure that those blooms she did bring into the house echoed her new colour schemes. The Red Hot Pokers were not her idea of a perfect house flower but they would bring life to a sadly neglected part of the garden.

She soon realized that Michael wanted nothing to do with her, as usual, and only wanted to lecture the boys – as usual. So she wandered out into the garden (her own special place). When Grace looked over the fence and saw her approaching, she rushed down her garden path and thrust a bucket into Jane's hands.

"Good! Now we can get on with the work," said the energetic old lady and led the way to the clump of overcrowded leaves at the back of her border. "Would you give me your arm for a minute, Jane, and I will step carefully over these primulas and into the thick of things."

"As the roots are for my benefit, Mrs Sanderson, I think I should be the one who goes into the foliage and does the digging," Jane smiled.

"But I'm quite capable."

"I know you are Mrs Sanderson but I would like to do it. I do enjoy gardening and this is the first time I have done any digging for months."

"Well, if you would like to, then go ahead," she said, accepting the fib.

Without another comment, Jane stepped carefully into the congestion and bent down to start removing some of the outer sections of the huge plant. Her efforts were so energetic that she had to remove her old coat and she wondered just how such a spindly old person like Grace would have survived this kind of activity, but she would and Jane knew she would have persevered until the job was done. She must have been in her late eighties or even nineties but showed the enthusiasm and energy of someone a third of her age.

"Now come and have a cup of tea, my dear", she said, holding out her hands for the heavy, full bucket of roots, which Jane deftly swung onto the grass and jumped over after it.

"I'm afraid not today. I must get on with my cooking, now that I've had my little foray into the garden. Perhaps another time and thank you for the Pokers." She saw Grace's face fall, as she came to terms with the fact that other people had more to do than dig up roots all day. It was such a pity that she lived alone. Jane wondered if she had any family and whether they came to visit as she had never seen another person go to Grace's front door.

She went back to her housework and cooking with a lighter heart and even enjoyed making the regulation evening meal. The amounts prepared had increased as the boys matured, so that she provided meals for four people now but the time and effort involved was no more than it had been and she enjoyed cooking in her new, large kitchen.

Having more to discuss this evening had made her look forward to Michael's return because she knew she could contribute to the conversation around the table. However, when she realised that he was going to be his usual reticent self, she was determined not to help him by introducing a new topic for him to decimate. Instead, she remained totally silent and allowed the boys to describe what had happened at school that day. When they all left the table and she was left to clear and wash up the dishes, her thoughts turned once more to the subjects which interested her, such as gardening, sewing and, much as she fought it, Rob.

000

The following day was fine and sunny and Jane was prepared to spend most of her time working in the garden. She donned her garden smock and rubber boots and tied a bright, cotton scarf around her neck, then made her way out to the small copse at the end of the back garden. For a while, she sat on the old mildewed bench under a big, old apple tree, with its thick branches and peered through the burgeoning foliage at the blue sky. If she could arrange for the boys to be with her, without Michael seeing them, she knew they would love to climb onto the solid branches, up into the density of the ancient tree. That's what boys did and to have the means for climbing here, in their own garden, was wonderful. There was the sweet sound of birdsong all around her and she particularly noted the mellifluous tones of the blackbird calling to another of its ilk in a distant tree. This was the time for mating and each bird sang its heart out, trying to attract a partner for the coming year. She knew some birds preferred to stay with one mate for life, while others searched afresh each spring but whatever, their singing created a sadness in Jane when she thought of her own mate and how their marriage had turned out. The only good things to emerge from their union were the boys. Oh how she wanted them to mature in loving and sympathetic surroundings and how she hated the way Michael debased them at every opportunity. It had been so pleasing to watch them relating to the warm, good-natured personality of Rob.

No matter where her thoughts began and how detached they were from him, her ruminations always closed with a vision of the strong figure of Rob Barclay. She was very aware that he was the only attractive male she knew at this bad time in her life but she did wish that she could divorce him from her everyday thoughts. Perhaps if she dissected his appearance deliberately, that would do it? So she started with his wavy hair of an indeterminate mousy colour. He wore it short cropped, no doubt due to the amount of work he did but the few times Jane had met him he had shown a tidy, shaven neckline above his unusually white, open-necked shirt. It was strange to see a gardener wearing such a pristine collarless shirt with a really scruffy, leather waistcoat but it helped to show off his brown, weathered facial skin. His body was solid and probably was muscular, as were his arms in his rolled-up sleeves, sporting that attractive fairish hair down to the backs of his manly, shapely hands. He wore heavy, corduroy trousers and boots like any working man and he walked casually erect, like someone who was used to covering ground quickly and effortlessly. Oh, here she goes again.

By the time she had studied her mental picture of Rob, Jane found herself breathing rapidly and heavily, so the exercise had done nothing to lighten her load, only serving to increase her longing to see this paragon once more. She was behaving like a schoolgirl who is smitten by her first sight of a handsome man and cannot get him out of her mind and that was not what she had intended.

The next method involved working as hard as she possibly could, so that the physical effort dispelled her mental image and this seemed to be more of a solution. She hoed and raked and weeded, until she was once more breathing heavily but this time it was due to her gardening activities and not to her mental state.

Feeling the back plot was looking much better, she ducked under the fresh leaves of the fruit trees and emerged at the front of the house, her hoe in hand ready to commence the formal borders. As she stood thinking and deliberating her next move, she happened to glance over the wall into Grace Sanderson's garden. There, in exactly the same pose, was Rob Barclay, staring through the shrubbery at her, his mouth slightly curled in his half-mocking smile. Jane's first impulse was to run back the way she had come but she felt this would show what effect he had on her, so she merely lifted her hand and waved, nonchalantly.

In return, Rob moved closer to the dividing wall and leaned through the bushes.

"Hello there. I was wondering if I would see you today. As I said previously, Mrs Sanderson likes me to do the heavy work in her garden and I thought you might like some roots of various perennials I am taking out."

This was a bonus. Not only did he do more than pass the time of day but there was a prize as well, which would save Grace from all that digging. What could she do?

"That would be very kind, Rob. I was wondering how I could introduce some colour into this predominantly green area, even though Grace gave me some roots of Red Hot Pokers recently. Just throw anything you don't want over the wall and I'll collect it later."

"Not at all, not at all. I'll bring a sackful round when I finish and leave it at your back door. That is, if you don't object."

I don't object, in the slightest, she thought, but what about Michael. If he caught sight of her gardening friend on their land, he was quite likely to throw him off. Jane realised that was the silliest thought she had had for years because Michael had no physical prowess whatsoever, whereas Rob ...

"No, that would be lovely," she said, smiling and wondering if she had hesitated for too long while she reflected on her husband. However, Rob did not appear to have noticed and said,

"I'll bring it round later, then. There's a bare space near the garage where I can stack plants."

He must know the garden to have said that. Maybe he had done some work for the previous occupant. After finishing her hoeing, she went back into the scullery and quickly changed her shoes. Then she went upstairs and combed her hair, biting hard on her lips to give them some colour, before dancing down the stairs and into the kitchen. She could hardly take her eyes off the window, as she waited for Rob to pass it with the bag of plants. When she did see him go by, her face began to flush and she took a rapid sip of water to cool herself down before going once more to the back door.

"Oh, thank you so much Rob, I do appreciate it," she said, feeling very unlike herself and realising that she was talking like Grace next door.

"That's quite alright, Madam," he said, looking directly at her with his mocking green eyes. He had noticed.

"I-I'm sorry, I meant... I mean I do appreciate your kindness. I'm just so unused to such treatment... I mean I... Thank you, Rob."

"What a performance about a few spare bits of root. I don't even know if they'll come to anything..." he said. The spare plants obviously meant nothing to him but to her they were like pieces of gold found in the river.

"Oh, they will. I'll see to that. They'll have the best treatment I can give them."

"I believe you. I do declare you could force anything to grow, just with your willpower!"

They both started to laugh and Jane was glad that her embarrassing moment had gone. She was rarely tongue-tied but Rob seemed to turn her into some kind of stammering idiot. Why was she being so ridiculous; perhaps it was because Michael made her feel so unattractive and Rob looked at her as he would look at any pretty woman. He was still talking.

"But just in case your magic doesn't work, I'll be back at the weekend and feel quite free to ask for some more. Now, I must put away Mrs Sanderson's lovely old tools and be on my way. Goodbye, Jane."

"Goodbye, Rob," she said and wondered how two words could be so totally miserable. At least he would be around at the weekend - but so would Michael. And she must ensure the two didn't meet.

CHAPTER 11

"Right. Today we will go to Bathgate and buy some curtain material," Michael said, on Saturday morning. "And I don't want to hear any complaints from either of you boys. You will help your mother to carry her packages back to the motorcar and we will all behave in a civilised fashion."

That will be an unusual occurrence, thought Jane as she tidied away the breakfast dishes and prepared to wash them up.

"That won't be necessary, either, Jane. You can do them when we come home. I will be going off to meet some of my friends, so you'll need something to keep you occupied." Just what she needed – washing up to fill in her time until he returned for his next meal. Instead of watching you read the newspaper or doing some housework, you mean, she thought. This life was one long scene from a play, with Jane speaking her part when required and also being the audience with her own idea of how the lines affected her. Only the children behaved naturally because they either did not know about the nuances hidden in their parents' conversations, or did not care.

But that thought wasn't quite true. Henry fastened his gaze on his father and then his mother, wondering what lies she was going to tell next. Father thought that if he ignored his sons they did not count as people and had no minds of their own and mother was so determined to make their life a happy one that she pretended all the time. Andrew was so scatterbrained and involved in his own pursuits that he never noticed anything. But Henry knew exactly what was going on.

"Off we go then!" Michael had decided to leave and there was an immediate rush for the hallstand to collect hats and coats. Jane was last into the car, pulling on gloves and straightening her coat lapels, moving her hair out of the way, as she climbed aboard, knowing that Michael would pick up on anything he felt was wrong about her. It was so easy to second-guess him.

The shopping trip was successful, if a little feverish and the material they bought was to her liking, for one reason; she had played a little game. Whenever she particularly liked a pattern or a fabric, she said how unsuitable it would be and Michael then approached an assistant to cut off the lengths they required. If she hated something, she became excited and enthused over it, as if she simply had to have it or die. The opposite reaction was that Michael walked away without a second look.

They reached the Austin, everyone except Michael laden with brown-paper packages and they were stuffed in the boot and in the back seat beside the boys. They had bought the thread and some fine needles and, despite the assistant asking if they would like the store sempstresses to make them up, Jane came away with her large packages, knowing how much work was involved. Michael thought the sewing would cost too much. And, of course, his wife had to have something to occupy her. Jane enjoyed sewing but not on such a large scale.

On arriving home, they were literally tipped out onto the drive and Michael drove away, without so much as a goodbye. It was long after lunchtime and Henry and Andrew were starving, so she went indoors to prepare a meal while the helpful two brought in the parcels.

She had not given a thought to Rob, knowing how he tried to finish any rough gardening work in the mornings and imagining that he would be long gone, so it was with some surprise that she saw his fair head pass the window. Henry was first to see him at the back door and felt himself smiling involuntarily when he was treated to a huge wink.

"Hello Henry. Is your mother in?"

"Yes, Rob. I'll get her for you," he said, feeling more pleased than he had for days.

When he pranced into the kitchen cheerfully and blurted out that

"Rob, the gardener, is looking for you Mother," Jane pretended to be surprised, although she had already groped in her handbag for a comb and a mirror.

"I wonder what he could want with me," she said.

"I don't know – he didn't say," smiled Henry and Jane thought how handsome he looked with his teeth showing and wondered why he didn't do it more often. Then she went to the door and invited Rob to come in.

"No thank you. I won't come in. I'm wearing dirty boots and I can see your floor is beautifully clean. I just wanted to know if you will be needing any more root cuttings because I'm about to throw my thinnings on the compost heap."

"I'm afraid I haven't had time to put the last lot in yet. They're still in a heap round the side."

"Oh dear, been a busy few days has it? In that case, let me put them in for you. Just come round and tell me where you want them and I'll get on with it now."

"Oh no! I couldn't allow that, Rob. You've done quite enough as it is."

"Nonsense. I can have them in before you've turned round. Anyway, I expect these young men keep you occupied at weekends."

"Oh dear. I don't know what you must think of me. I fully intended to plant the Red Hot Pokers on Thursday and to continue with the others the next day."

"Don't give it another thought. This is my job remember. I will be much quicker than you, anyway."

"I don't want you to think I'm taking advantage of you, Rob. I really did intend to plant the roots."

Many another man would have turned her comment into innuendo but not Rob. He merely smiled and turned away, to the heap of greenery by the side of the garage wall. Remembering what she was doing, Jane called him back and said,

"I'm making some late lunch for the boys. Would you like to come in and have some soup and cheese?"

"No thank you. I won't impose upon you."

"See it as my thank you for what you're doing for me," she said, smiling.

"Well, I haven't had anything to eat since breakfast – but I won't come in. Would you mind giving me a piece of bread and some cheese out here?"

It felt like handing out charity to the poor but Jane made up some bread and butter and a big slab of cheese, taking it to the back door. And Rob grinned and tipped his head as though tipping his cap. She would have liked him to come in and eat with them at the table but realised that this would be totally wrong. Where had her morals gone? What if Michael were to return unexpectedly? At least Rob understood and had behaved correctly.

After feeding her hungry children and taking a bite herself, she could hardly keep her eyes from the front garden. She had walked out the front door and shown Rob where she anticipated placing her new plants for the best effect, feeling like one of the 'toffs' he had talked about. There was no doubt about it – there was a social gap between them like the Forth River, now that she lived in a big house in Ecclesmachan.

000

Time rattled on, as her Singer treadle sewing machine did and Michael came home from work and pricked her sensibilities just as much as her sharp needle pricked her finger when she came to turning up the hems on the miles of curtain material. However, after working like a factory girl for several weeks, the marathon task was over and Jane climbed the step-ladder and hung up the finished items.

How different the rooms looked and how warm they felt, now the sun was shining with more strength on the windows. It was almost July and she had spent the best part of the early summer indoors, so she planned to take a walk now that the job was done.

Following a similar route to the one she had taken with her sons, all those months ago, as she was hitching up her skirt to climb the fence into the scrub, there was a loud 'parp' from a vehicle coming down the hill. She almost fell, as she looked round to see Rob's van on the other side of the road and, without more ado, he parked it on the grassy verge and ran across.

"It's a grand day for rambling!" he said, glancing at her precarious position on top of the fence.

"I just had to have a walk in the fresh air," she replied, jumping down on the other side. "I seem to have been sewing curtains for years – and now they're all finished, I thought I deserved a break."

"You certainly do. Would you mind if I accompany you for a while. I need a bit of relaxation as well."

"It's a strange way for a gardener to relax, isn't it?" she chuckled.

"Well, it's not so much a sit down I need; just some company that will talk back to me. I spend so much time with pieces of foliage and flowers that I forget how to converse."

"In that case, come along. We can chat as we go."

They wandered along the grassy path, until they reached a stile leading into a field and Jane fully expected him to turn back, having left the van on the roadside, but he leapt over and held out his hand.

CHAPTER 12

Having talked non-stop about the surrounding villages and Rob's clients, they were both breathless as they skirted round a herd of cows and headed for the burn where they had been drinking. In the heat, the whole area smelled of cow-dung and a little way along the muddy embankment, the path took a turn over another stile until they were faced with one of the small shale bings.

"Oh dear, I hate these blots on the landscape," Jane said.

"I know what you mean but they were made in a very good cause. Think of all the work that came to the area due to the discovery of oil under the ground."

"But it seems such a pity that these tips weren't taken away and used in some way."

"Perhaps one day they will be but there wasn't the manpower to do such a tidy job, after all the hard work involved in extracting the oil. Do you know, it all began when a coalmaster from Wishaw was granted mining rights in this area and he found oil-bearing rock as well as coal. Of course you know about the mining for oil everywhere around here – you must have grown up with it. My father was one of the last men to be paid off at the Broxburn Refinery."

"Oh really. Have you always lived here? Whereabouts did your family stay?"

Rob ignored her comment, and suddenly pointed across the field to a heron flying low over the golden corn and said,

"What a wonderful sight. They are such massive birds. Look at his wing span. I expect he's just come out of the burn where he was fishing for his dinner."

Jane wondered whether his change of subject had been deliberate or whether he had just spotted the huge bird. Anyway, she let the subject of his family go for now. They found a large rock and sat down for a rest and she found herself wanting him to sit closer when she felt the warmth of his thigh against hers. Just the close proximity of another human being was comforting. She looked right into his eyes and said,

"I find all this farmland so beautiful, don't you?"

He remained staring at her for several seconds and then, impulsively, he leaned forward and kissed her full on the mouth. Nothing was said by either of them and there was no repetition. Instead, Rob rose and held out his hand to Jane, to pull her onto her feet.

"I'm sorry, Jane, I shouldn't have done that," he said, somewhat sadly.

"It's alright, Rob."

"I do understand that you're a married woman and I don't usually take advantage like that. It will never happen again."

"It's alright," she said again and thought she had better make it clear that she did not usually behave in such a promiscuous fashion either. "It was probably the effect of the sun and the warm weather. Think nothing of it" and she smiled as she brushed down her skirt. The only trouble was that she wanted it to happen as much as he did. How could she say think nothing of it, when she desperately wanted him to think a great deal of it? But the moment had passed and they were once more striding across the field towards the pathway. The only trouble was he had left her with an unbearable yearning for his nearness, the warmth of his hard body, his kisses.

"I think I will leave you here, Jane and get back to my van," he said, breaking the spell.

"Yes, I intend to walk into the village before going home. It was so good to see you, Rob." She wondered whether he would take her hand or make some kind of contact but he acted as though nothing had happened and they parted company, leaving her alone with her thoughts.

Jane was left with such an unbearable feeling of anticlimax as she continued down the narrow lane. There was new growth by the sides of the path, of docken, ragwort and buttercups but it all melted into the mist of her unshed tears. The leaves and blossoms of the hawthorn and elder bushes caught her shoulders as she jumped the tiny brook and left the friendly shelter of the wild area. Now it was farm track, scattered with puddles which she avoided, jumping from one side to the other, until she reached the village and civilisation. Her mind was in turmoil, so that she passed people she knew with little more than a brief smile. All she wanted to do was go home and hide herself away, until these strange emotions left her.

At least her brisk walk back along the Ecclesmachan Road served to clear out some of the dross from her mind and she was able to turn into her own drive with a clear conscience and a definite idea of what she would do in future.

000

There was no need for Jane to take her moral stance because a few days later she received news from Grace that Rob had left his job and gone off to the big city. Seemingly, he had a friend who worked at the Botanical Gardens in Edinburgh and he had cajoled him into saying a few words in the right ear, with the result that he had been taken on as a jobbing gardener during their busy season.

It was sad that he had left without a goodbye but half of Jane was glad that she no longer had to face the temptation of his presence; the other half missed him dreadfully. However, having decided that she would never encourage him again, this was just another of those tricks of destiny which would work out for the best, no doubt.

That very Friday, Michael came home from work, seething. He grabbed Jane by the arm and thrust her up against the kitchen wall, not stopping to notice that she was holding a sharp meat cleaver in her hand. She had been about to chop through a crown of lamb to make chops for their evening meal and only just stopped herself from bringing it down hard on his head.

Instead, she dropped it onto the stone floor and heard the loud clang, as her head was shoved back onto the hard wall.

"What the hell have you been doing now, my lady?" said Michael in a soft, grim voice, which could only mean that he was furious.

"I don't know what you mean," she tried to mumble, through the fingers of his hand.

"You don't know! You don't know! Surely you know when you take a nice little stroll through the woods with your friend, the gardener!"

Oh God, somebody must have seen them. Thank Goodness Rob had left the area, at least during the day. She managed to lift her head and shift his hand away from her mouth but now it was round her throat and she knew he was quite capable of throttling her.

"Tell me what you mean. I can't explain anything, if I don't know what you're talking about, can I?" she cried out, hysterically.

"You've been spotted, by one of my men, in the company of that wastrel, the one with the filthy motor, the one who does you so many favours around the garden. I was casually informed at lunchtime that my own wife was seen walking through the shrubbery with the man who purports to help you out with the garden. Is that all he helps you out with?! Answer me and don't even think of lying. Remember where my hand is resting, if you would!"

"You've got it all wrong, Michael. I took a walk, to clear my head after I'd sewn all those curtains and I happened to meet Rob on the road. He needed to stretch his legs and we walked along together, that's all."

"I don't believe a word of it. You arranged to meet him. Go on, admit it. You arranged your little meeting, knowing how secluded it is near the bing. It's just unlucky for you that Alec has to walk his dog there sometimes and spotted you."

As long as he did not see what happened when they sat down. Please, please, don't let him mention that. Michael was quite capable of killing her for such a misdemeanour.

"There was nothing to spot. I walked along with the gardener for a little while, then he went back to the main road and I continued my walk. Surely, you wouldn't want me to ignore people, just because we live in the biggest house in the village." She knew this would appeal to his vanity.

"Living in a big house only means you have to be more careful of your behaviour. You can't continue to appear like a slut when you live in the big house."

He was calming down. He said 'continue' so he must think she was a slut in the past. She could even feel his fingers relaxing slightly. If she could only pander to his arrogant nature a little more, all could still be well.

"I'm sorry, Michael. I'm not practised at living like the gentry, not like you. I will try harder."

He released her neck and then did something which frightened her even more. He bent down and picked up the cleaver from the floor. Her breathing stopped. She was sure she was about to faint and then he turned away, the horrible implement still in his hand. It could only have been moments before he replaced the butcher's knife on the work surface but, to Jane, it felt like hours.

"You should be careful with items like this; they can hurt people you know," he said, with a cruel smile and then turned back to her and pushed his face forward, so their eyes were close together. "Don't imagine you could ever get away with any hanky-panky. My spies are everywhere."

Jane could hardly wait until he left the room. She grabbed a kitchen stool and sat down heavily, rubbing her throat where he had clutched her so tightly and when she looked into the small mirror in the back passage, she saw his fingerprints in red, now turning to blue. She was dripping with sweat, due to not knowing what was going to happen to her, from the fear of what he might be prompted to do with the cleaver. And all this had happened now Rob had departed. What a good thing he had. Or was it? She had no-one to tell. She had no-one. The feeling of lonely hopelessness and her past foolishness made her break down into a tearful mess and this is how her boys saw her when they returned from having tea with their friends.

To add to everything that had gone before, she now felt dreadfully guilty and tried to gloss over it by saying she had dropped the meat on the floor. Had they believed her? Probably not.

CHAPTER 13

Henry knew that something dreadful was happening to his family. For years he had crept out of bed to sit on the stairs, listening to the sarcastic, frightening comments thrown at his mother by his father. Until the time he first heard them arguing, he had imagined their life to be the same as other families and hoped the row was a single occurrence but his subconscious mind encouraged him to wake up a couple of hours after he went to sleep and he became fascinated yet horrified by the constant taunting and jeering which took place at the foot of the stairs.

He was now aware that it was his father who began the tirades of verbal abuse and his mother merely replied in a quieter vein but it was hard to know that the two people he loved most in the world were not on good terms, did not even like each other. Why did grown-ups have to make their children suffer like this? But that was a ridiculous thought because neither of them knew he was there, peering through the banisters into the dark, shivering in his striped pyjamas. It would have been so easy to be like Andrew and tuck himself up into bed, with his head under the blankets but he was unable to tear himself away. There were times when he wondered if his father would pick up a weapon and kill his mother. There were plenty of walking sticks and canes in the hallstand. What would he do then? He could hardly run down in his bare feet and fight off a strong man with his own hands – and he was his father after all. Eventually the tirade would cease and Henry had to clamp a hand over his mouth to stop himself from yawning into the vacuum created by the lack of noise. He crept silently back to his room and crawled into his bed, shaking like a leaf as if it were winter. He even wished he could have a hot water bottle but knew how foolish that would seem to his mother in the morning, when she came to straighten his bed. He tried to think about something beautiful, like the colours of a male pheasant, to take his mind off his troubles but, as soon as he had a picture of the brown, red and tan bird, he pictured a tweed-clad shooter raising his gun and picking off the fine fellow. He fell asleep watching the gorgeous creature falling to the ground.

Night after night Henry continued his surveillance, and it became a habit for him to crawl to the stairs, even when he was half asleep. He felt it was only due to his watchfulness that his mother was still alive and he dared not stop.

000

Summer was soon at an end and the autumn colours in the garden were just as attractive as those of the flowering season. Trees gradually took on their mantles of gold and russet and lost them to the high winds which came in October, so there was a carpet of brightly-coloured leaves from the back door to Grace's wall. They were allowed to help his mother pick apples which were right at the top of the tree. She collected those that dropped of their own accord; also the wind-falls for making into stewed apple. When the boys threw down their finds, Jane had to dodge to avoid being bashed on the head, which sent them into peals of laughter. This was what being a mother was all about.

The boys learned that they could climb up onto the flat top of the boundary and carefully totter along like tightrope walkers, from one end to the other, now that most of the leaves had left the shrubs on the dividing line. Jane knew that boys did this kind of thing to prove their bravery to themselves and their peers but, nonetheless, she stood with bated breath at the window while the daring exhibition was taking place. One day, she happened to glance to the left and noticed Grace at her own window, her hand held up to shade her eyes from the glare of the low autumn sun.

It was sad that she had no sons or daughters to visit her in her old age and even sadder that she had missed all the joy of seeing a child of her own turning into an adult. What must it be like? A life wasted – and yet someone without children was freer than a parent; there would be none of the small worries like that of today, none of the irritations which filled in the day, none of the happiness. Yes, life without a child would be like life without the sun.

As Jane watched the pixie-like face at the window over the wall, there was a twitching of the curtain and a brown and white fluffy body appeared on Grace's shoulder. Without hesitation, she turned and planted a kiss on the small head and Jane knew that, for Grace, her cats had taken the place of children. She had two small bundles of fur, one sleek and grey and the one she saw now. They were often in the garden, stalking some unsuspecting mouse or bird but Jane hadn't the heart to chase them. This had most probably been their territory for years and she knew the law of the wild applied to the domestic cat more than any other pet animal.

000

Grace let down her lace curtain and sat down, Lucy still on her shoulder. It was good to see those boys next door having adventures in the garden. She had never been blessed with children, mainly because her husband was so much older than she and had not seemed to be interested in the passionate side of life.

She had been his secretary in Edinburgh and had seen him through the death of his wife, ensuring that he was comforted when necessary and forming a protective wall around him, which kept other lawyers and some dizzy clients away from the office. As a result, when all the formalities of the funeral were over (which Grace organised, more or less single-handedly) he asked her to walk out with him and then, some time later, proposed marriage. It was all done very quietly and tastefully, much to the chagrin of his daughter from his previous union. She had not liked Grace at all, seeing her as an interloper and, Grace thought, imagining that she only wanted Maurice for his house and his money. This could not have been further from her mind; she admired the man and respected him, seeing in him all she had missed from a father. Hers had died at sea when she was an infant and her mother followed him a few years later, from grief they said. Grace was brought up by her granny, who had lived in this very house in Ecclesmachan and she had attended a dame's school in Edinburgh, in the way of all well-brought-up girls, according to Granny.

Her early life had been sheltered and her character had been moulded by someone who was Victorian in every way. The house had been draped with satin and lace; the piano legs were covered for modesty and large plants were in every spare corner. There were paintings covering each wall and the woodwork was dark and shiny. Each door had a curtain on brass rails above it, to keep out the draughts, and every window was shielded in lace.

After their marriage, Maurice wanted her to move into town to live in his large, stone-built terraced house on the south side of Edinburgh but she refused, so strongly that he was forced to move into the country, or lose his wife. It came at about the right time for both of them because Maurice had been debating retirement from his law firm for some time and he decided to combine it with his separation from city life. His Edinburgh house was sold and the money held in his own bank account.

Once they were ensconced in the village, their house appeared like something from an antique dealer's catalogue and they were forced to sell many items, in order to make themselves comfortable. This did not please the daughter and she refused to speak to her father from that day until his death. Maurice was heartbroken to lose his only daughter and even said, on his deathbed, that he held no hard feelings and that, in his will, she would receive all his remaining possessions, leaving only the house to Grace, which had belonged to her anyway. This left Grace feeling extremely miserable, as she knew that her care for him in his final years must have meant nothing to him.

So, without a husband and without a child, she reverted to her old ways and only slightly modernised her grandmother's house.

000

Jane's doorbell was ringing, most persistently. She had decided to wash her hair and was sitting near the hearth, brushing out her fair tresses for the fire to dry it. The only time she dared to light a fire was when Michael was at work, or when visitors were expected. He expected her to keep warm by working in the house or garden and pointed out that the boys had plenty of warm jerseys to wear if they were cold.

She brushed her shoulder-length hair, so that it was tidy and tucked it behind her ears, before rushing to the front door to see what was so urgent. There, in a dreadful state, was Grace and

Jane could swear that she saw tears in her eyes under her spectacles.

"Oh, thank Heavens you're at home, Jane. I am quite faint with worry. My grey pussy, Georgie, came in this morning from his night-time hunting, in the most dreadful state. His ear was bleeding profusely and he was unable to breathe properly. Please, please, would you come and look at him and help me to call out the vet.?"

"Of course I will, Grace. Just come in for a moment while I put on some suitable clothes. As you can see, I have just washed my hair and I'm not looking my best."

CHAPTER 14

"Oh, don't worry about that my dear. Just come and see Georgie. I'm at my wits' end."

"Now, don't worry. I'll be back in a cat's whis... oh, I'm sorry. I mean I won't be long. You just sit down there and wait for me."

"No. No. I can't do that. I must get back to him. He will think his mother has deserted him. I'll go back and you follow when you can."

She went out, shuffling and sniffing, not looking around once and Jane feared for her safety because she moved so quickly for an old person. Once she had seen her out of the door, down the couple of steps and on the way to the gate, she hared up her stairs two at a time and found a jumper and some shoes. Then she rushed downstairs and out, remembering too late that she had slammed the door locked without picking up her house keys. She would have to think about that later.

Grace had left the door open for her and she cooeed as she entered. There was a feeble call from a room at the end of the hallway and Jane guessed that the layout of the house would be similar to her own and that it would be the kitchen. She quickly closed the door behind her and made her way down the dark passage to an entrance on the right. She hardly noticed the old furniture as she rushed along but a huge grandfather clock began to strike the hour as she passed it, making her jump in surprise and gaze at the large white face, bearing pictures around the edges; two brass pendulums moved around in the glass-fronted panel of the mahogany casing, while the rest of the clock reverberated from the two loud dongs.

"Oh there you are my dear girl. Just come and look at my precious pussy. He certainly seems to have been in the wars, doesn't he?"

On the work surface was a cardboard box lined with pale green blanket and lying in this nest was the grey cat, heaving as he tried to breathe and looking as if something had tried to bite his head off, let alone his ear. At first glance, Jane held out no hopes for the survival of such a badly mauled animal but she was unable to say these words to Grace and said,

"He doesn't look well at all, Grace. Where is the telephone number for the vet and I will call him?"

"I'm sorry, dear. I don't have a telephone. I have no time for all this modern nonsense. I was going to run down to the surgery on the Uphall corner myself but now I don't feel he should be left."

"Don't worry, Grace. I will go and call from my telephone. It will be much quicker than walking down the road."

It certainly would be. The road was almost a mile long. So, Jane rushed out the way she had come and tramped across the pebbles to her own front door. It was then that she remembered locking the door as she left. Surely, there would be an open window on the ground floor somewhere, or one she could prize open with a knife from the garden. With this thought in mind, she raced from window to window, only to find them all securely fastened. What was she to do now? Run to the village as Grace had suggested – no, there was one other idea.

She knew there was a bathroom window open, just above a flat, jutting piece of roof for the dining room window and she knew it would push up in order for her to climb in but to do this she would need a ladder. There was one in the garage. All she had to do was carry it round to the back of the house.

It was a double ladder, provided for inspecting the guttering and therefore heavy but it was the only way, so she heaved it out of the dark interior and made her way slowly towards the back door. By propping it up, she managed to climb onto the little flat roof and from there it was easy to manhandle the sash window open enough to climb inside. If she thought her troubles were over, she was wrong because the wash basin was directly under the window and the only way to manoeuvre herself into the room was to slide full-length on her stomach, but she did it, knocking her arms on the taps.

Once in the house, the first thing she did was to run downstairs and grab the forgotten keys, pushing them into her skirt pocket as if they were valuable treasure. She would be able to come home in the normal way, at least. Her next act was to pick up the telephone and ask the operator for the number Grace had given her. Thank goodness, the vet was there and he promised to drive straight up.

Jane's breathing was almost as laboured as Georgie's, as she looked down at her dishevelled appearance. Her navy-blue skirt was creased beyond imagining and marked down the front with long, white lines – of the soap in the washbasin no doubt. Her stockings were laddered horribly in several places and there were loops of thread hanging from her fine, woollen sweater. A quick glance in the mirror, showed her a face marked with dirt and smudged lipstick; in fact she looked as if she had crawled through the proverbial hedge backwards. It was a matter of minutes before she had flung off all the offending clothing and wrapped herself unceremoniously in others dragged from her chest of drawers. The face would have to be satisfied with a quick rub around with a flannel.

She then remembered the keys and transferred them from one pocket to another before racing back to Grace and pretending that everything had gone according to plan. There was no need to add to the worries of the old lady by telling her her own mawkish story.

In little more than fifteen minutes, the vet was on the doorstep and Jane ushered him into the kitchen. As he followed her along the hallway, he mumbled something about being surprised that either of the cats were still alive, then noisily cleared his throat before marching in to Grace.

"Now, Mrs Sanderson, what have we here?" he said in his Edinburgh accent.

"Oh, doctor," she said. "Come and have a look at poor pussy. He was out all night and must have had a fight because he came back this morning like this. Please say you can put him right."

The vet stood back and took a look, then moved in closer and felt around Georgie's feeble little body, before turning to the kitchen sink, where he carefully washed his hands and dried them on a towel handed to him by Grace.

"I'm afraid you're going to have to brace yourself, Mrs Sanderson. There's no easy way to say this. He's come to the end of his life span. By far the kindest thing I can do is to give him an injection and put him out of his misery now, this minute."

Jane looked at Grace and fully expected her to burst into tears but she just stared into the vet's eyes, took a deep breath and said,

"You know best, doctor. I only want what's best for pussy."

"Do you want to go into the other room while I dispatch the wee fella? I'm sure your friend here will keep you company?"

"No. I can't let him think I'm deserting him in his hour of need," she said, completely dry-eyed. "I want to hold him close while you do the deed. Will you pass him up to me, he's a bit heavy for me to carry and not hurt him?"

Jane was quite amazed, particularly after the frenzy that had presaged the vet's appearance but she was full of admiration for the slim, little old lady, who was wearing her bravest expression and holding herself as erect as her bent body would allow. The rugged, old vet. went across to the box and carefully lifted the now noisily heaving animal, passing him tenderly across to Grace, who sat in a rocking chair near the window. Without hesitating for a moment, he picked a syringe out of his bag, filled it from a bottle, tapped it and pressed it gently into the folds of flesh on Georgie's stomach.

"This will take a minute or two. Just talk to him and stroke him, Mrs Sanderson and he'll feel content."

Grace did exactly as she was told, muttering endearments to her tormented pet, until the heavy breathing slowed then stopped. She was left holding a limp, grey bundle.

"It's alright Georgie," she whispered. "You'll be with God in a minute and I'll see you soon."

Jane tried to stop herself from crying but the tears cascaded down her face and she had to turn away and surreptitiously wipe her face. When she looked back at the others, they were still standing, as if in a tableau, the only movement in the scene was the gentle trickle of tears down the passive, weathered face of the old vet. Grace remained true to her name, gazing down at her now drooping pussy.

Clearing his throat several times, the vet. said, "Let me take him from you, my dear. Would you like me to take him away with me."

"No! No! He must have a proper burial. I must be sure it's done properly!" Then, feeling she had been rude to a venerated member of the medical profession, she became apologetic and said, "No, doctor. I like to bury my cats myself. It's a long time since I had to do it but I have a special place in the garden, under my Albertine rose where Georgie will lie at rest. Thank you. Thank you very much for all you have done. It can't be easy."

"No, Mrs Sanderson, it isn't easy but it has to be done to avoid our animals being in pain. I'm sorry to spring this on you. I hope you understand, my dear."

Grace nodded and smiled sweetly at the retreating man and Jane followed him to the front door, feeling like the butler.

"She a tough 'un that," he said. "I wish there were more like her in this world. We get so many women hanging on to their dying animals for purely selfish reasons."

Jane felt nothing more could be said, so followed Grace's example and nodded, then smiled and the vet walked off to his motorcar, bag in hand. She knew that Grace would have to give in to her emotions some time and wondered if she should stay to keep her company in her obvious grief but the decision was completely taken out of her hands.

"Now, my dear friend. You must get back to your family. It's about the time your dear boys come home from school and I'm sure you have a meal to make for your dinner."

"Well, I'm quite happy to stay with you, if you would like."

"No. Everything has been done that could be done. I must thank you for all your help today. I could not have done it without you. The only thing left to do now is to bury my little pussy in the back garden. Perhaps you would come over tomorrow and help me to dig a hole. I will get him ready."

"O…of course. When shall I come? In the morning sometime. I will pop in when the boys go off to school."

It was the last thing that Jane had envisaged – officiating at the funeral of a cat – but Grace was such a kind old soul that she knew she would go and do whatever was necessary. Having planned the sad task for tomorrow, she left Grace alone with her sorrow and went home.

CHAPTER 15

As she turned into her drive, the boys were coming along the road and ran to greet her. Then she remembered the ladder. She was sure she could trust them to be tactful and asked them if they would help her to put it back in the garage. Three pairs of hands made the job so much easier and Henry and Andrew were amazed when she told them her story. Finishing by saying, I would count it a favour if you kept this tale to yourselves, she glimpsed a look of understanding in the eyes of her older boy, who immediately looked down at his shoes while they both agreed and said, yes of course. And she knew Henry would insist that Andrew kept his mouth shut.

The following morning, a lidded and padded cardboard box, wrapped in birthday paper, was lowered gently into an earthy grave at the foot of Grace's Albertine rose. Jane took a spade and covered it over with soil, while Grace said a few words of prayer and they both went back to the house for a cup of tea and a piece of Victoria sponge. In the middle of the funeral repast, Lucy the fluffy one wandered in and looking calmly around, jumped up on Grace's lap, to be invited to partake of a few crumbs.

"I still have my baby, you see," Grace whispered and Jane just nodded, knowing for a fact that the baby was about fifteen years old.

CHAPTER 16

Rob walked down a long road on the outskirts of Edinburgh, gazing around at the trees beyond iron palings and thinking how rural this part of the city appeared, away from the hurly-burly of the main thoroughfares. He had been offered a room in his friend's little house in Leith and it was a mere twenty minutes' walk to get to work from there. Although he called Alistair a friend, he was in fact a distant cousin on his mother's side and the family ties obviously did the trick when he had asked him about work in Edinburgh. Putting in a good word for him with the head gardener had been a great favour but Alistair saw it as the natural way to treat a relative.

The Royal Botanic Gardens were well-established in Inverleith and had become a popular venue for city dwellers who had no gardens of their own and wished to savour the delights of the countryside. Rob knew from Alistair that the idea of 'The Botanics', as it was known, had devolved from the existence of a physic garden in the 17th century, to study plants used in medicine, which was moved about the city of Edinburgh before they found the most suitable place. It was only after a petition had been signed to open the present gardens to the public, initially after church every Sunday, that it had become such a popular landmark. There were so many gardeners employed throughout the seventy acres, handling major jobs such as seed planting and cutting back spent flowers and foliage that it had been a simple task for Alistair to suggest his cousin at a time when one of the number retired.

As Rob reached the tall, wrought iron gates, he had a feeling of imprisonment but this soon passed, when he realised how much space had been allotted to the project. There were trees and shrubs as far as the eye could see and beds of flowers at every turn. It was even better than working in large private gardens where, unfortunately, he could always see fences and the owner's house.

He had been told to report to a particular area for instructions and some initial training, so he made his way along a path which seemed to head in the right direction. There were plants in full bloom along his way and young trees, as well as mature giants, so he found himself in front of a huge glasshouse in no time at all. This must be the famous Palm House which had been constructed in 1850 to contain some of the exotic plants brought back from the wilds of foreign countries by Victorian searchers. How amazing to live in a country where these incredible trees grew naturally, with leaves as big as a child, growing from trunks of heavily textured bark.

He was soon at the business area, where potting sheds were tacked onto the sides of stone buildings and several men wearing grubby trousers and matching waistcoats over their collarless shirts seemed to be heading off to their work. One or two thrust caps onto their heads as they walked away chatting and laughing together. This was all new to Rob. He had never worked with anyone else and hoped he would be given time to investigate alone and not have to converse all day.

"Hey, lad!" an older man called from the doorway of one of the sheds. "Are you my new man, the one that was recommended by Alistair?"

"Aye," he said quietly.

"Well, come on in lad and let's see what we can give you to do the day."

Rob was glad this was a friendly man. At least he wasn't working for a misery face. He strode towards the open door and the man inside said,

"Shut it behind you, lad. We'll have a wee chat before you get your hands dirty."

When he left the brightness of the morning and shut the door behind him, he wondered fleetingly what he was doing with himself. After all, life hadn't been so hard on him so far. The gardening jobs he had done at home had been easy enough, if not particularly interesting but that business with the lass Jane had really got to him. Yes, he'd done the right thing. He'd had to get away.

As his eyes got used to the darkness, he could see an old table at the far side of a room which was filled with pots and boxes. Directly in front of him, the man who had called to him was perched on an upturned tea chest, his feet on a large plant pot and he was grinning to himself.

"OK, my man. I know what you're thinking. This is meant to be the Royal Botanics, so why isn't everybody looking spruced up and why is this character sitting with his hands in his pockets and his feet on a pot. Well, I'll tell you why, lad. It's because I'm the boss. Just you remember that and we'll get on like a house on fire. The only men who get their marching orders from old Jock are the slackers and them who forget who's the boss. Do you get me?"

"Aye."

"Do you never say anything but aye, lad? I haven't heard another syllable come out your mouth. Tell me what you've been doing this far. Maybe you can say a bit more than aye when you tell me."

So Rob gave old Jock the run down of his gardening experience and when he had finished, the Head Gardener seemed perfectly satisfied because he took his chin out of his hand and looked Rob straight in the eye, saying,

"There's more to you than meets the eye, if you'll pardon the pun, lad. I think you and me'll get on fine and dandy. Now, I'll put you in the hands of one of my assistants and see how you get on. Come along wi' me, lad."

That was all there was to it and Rob was introduced to one of the Assistant Head Gardeners – a man called Graeme – who showed him where to pick up his tools and his uniform, which was the kit he had seen on the men leaving the courtyard. He was taken to a bed of mixed annuals and perennials and told to cut back everything that had flowered and uproot any annuals, before the dinner break. Graeme moved off, having a quick word with the gardener on the next bed before he went. Rob knew from the nods and gestures in his direction that the man was being told to keep an eye on him.

At lunch time, he made his way with several others to the cobbled courtyard and noticed that Alistair was already there.

"Hello, my man! Have you enjoyed your first morning with the elite?"

"Aye, that I have. It's no different from doing Mrs Meikle's plot, except I get to stop for my dinner."

"Well, get used to it because we always have a wee blether with our piece."

"That's better than a quick craik with a clump o' daisies. I've been so used to being on my own that I've started talking to the plants."

"Forget all that from now on, Rob. You'll need to know a bit about the big wide world if you're going to work with this clever lot. Let me introduce you to a few pals" and he did the rounds of the group of men perched around the yard. Rob knew he would have no chance of remembering the names of many of them unless he came into direct contact during the day but he went around shaking hands as they were thrust out. It all had the feeling of being decidedly friendly though and he planned to make the most of it.

CHAPTER 17

Back in Ecclesmachan, Jane realised that Grace had not bothered to get anyone else to help her in her garden, since Rob had departed. She mentioned this and was told,

'There's not much to do these days. I think I can manage myself.' Of course Jane knew this was impossible and decided to ask one of her boys to mow the lawns at the weekends. Grace was extremely grateful and rushed out on each occasion with a plate full of cakes and biscuits and a glass of orange juice. As it was Henry who had offered his services, he regularly came home with a pocketful of uneaten food, which he tossed to the birds, and Jane wondered which plant had benefited from a watering with fruit juice. He was a strange boy and tended to refuse anything which was offered to him by anyone outside the family but he was also a kind person and would hate to hurt Grace's feelings.

Jane did some weeding and tying-in of wayward stems next door, after she had finished her own gardening, so the two plots became one in her mind. She always found she was so full of energy in the garden and could dig and plant all day if necessary.

While she worked away in Grace's plot, the vision of Rob would appear to her, in the borders, under the shrubs on his hands and knees, carrying a sack full of weeds and cuttings to his battered van, even lifting his hand in greeting. This ghost followed her around in fine, sunny weather or in dismal, grey misty haars, even when she deliberately forced herself to think of other things, such as what she would cook for the evening meal or how she could help Grace to plan her garden to make it less tiring to maintain. Rob had certainly had an effect on her and now he had gone; run off, she guessed, to avoid further personal contact, but why? Perhaps he was a married man; she knew nothing about him. Surely, Grace would have heard some gossip and warned her off, but the old lady seemed to like him a great deal and had even encouraged Jane to be friendly with him. How could she find out where he was? His cottage was in the village and she had walked past it recently, only to find it looking neat and tidy, with curtains at the windows, as if someone had merely gone out shopping. If he had taken the trouble to do his own garden and retain his house, that must mean he planned to return sometime.

Here she went again. Rob, Rob, Rob. It was a sensible, manly name, Robert or perhaps it was Robin. After all the robin was known as the gardener's friend, so that would be quite appropriate but he looked more like a Robert. Why Rob and not Rab, as so many Scotsmen were called, after Rabbie Burns no doubt.

She was snipping and moving away tall pieces of eryngium from underneath a beautifully colourful holly tree. There were so many berries that she doubted there would be any left in a suitable condition for Christmas, particularly as she knew a group of starlings could denude such a tree in under an hour. Having been lost in thought, she had done much more of the winter clean-up than she had intended and she was now faced with a huge pile of mock thistles, which she would have to carry across to the compost heap. Luckily, Grace had allowed them to spread over a sizeable area, so there were very few weeds on the ground and Jane told herself that her work next week would be much lighter as a result of today's industry.

As she backed out of the flower bed, she saw the sprightly figure of Grace coming towards her, a cup and saucer in her hand. Because she was concentrating on not spilling the steaming hot liquid, she was not moving as quickly as usual, keeping her eyes on the tea.

"Oh Grace, you shouldn't have bothered," Jane said, knowing how facile such a comment sounded in the garden. It was the kind of thing you said when a near stranger gave you a birthday present, after being invited to dinner.

"Of course I should. I thought you were working as hard as Rob used to and I always used to bring him a cup of tea and his favourite, a Digestive biscuit, so here you are and I'm so proud of myself for not spilling a single drop."

"What a lovely treat. I hope you have had one indoors?"

"Yes, I've already had mine but I have to admit I brought out two Digestives, so I can join you in a snack."

"Good. Let me put my old jacket down on the bench and we can sit in comfort together."

They positioned themselves side by side on the old wooden seat, which had once been painted pale green but was now a mass of peeling paint, showing the old, faded coat of white underneath. Jane gazed around the garden, admiring the lovely old plants and wondering how long it would be before her own plot became as full and attractive.

"I know you miss him," Grace said.

"Miss who?" she replied, knowing full well who she meant but not wanting to admit it.

"Robert, of course." So he was a Robert and not a small bird, after all. "I miss him as well. He had become part of the garden to me. Such a helpful and cheerful young man. He would do anything for me. All I had to do was hint at something and the next week it would be done – and done extremely well. None of your botched jobs for Rob"

"I know. I learned a lot about gardening from him, without his ever telling me directly. I just copied his way of working. I do miss him, Grace, and I often wonder what has become of him."

"Oh, didn't I tell you my dear. He's taken a job at the Botanics in Edinburgh. Seemingly, his cousin worked there and put his name forward."

"But his cottage – it looks as if he still lives there... I mean, I walked past it the other day... he told me where he lives... about his garden, I mean."

"He plans to return in the winter months. After Christmas, I believe and he drops in to keep the place looking spick and span, while he's staying in Leith. I don't think we've seen the last of Robert but I don't expect he will want to return to my old garden, not after he's seen all the wonderful plants in the physic garden."

Jane knew the Botanics had been started as a physic garden for the medicinal herbs used by doctors of old, remembering what her mother had told her about the various moves made for the gardens in the city of Edinburgh, from a plot the size of a handkerchief to the massive collection of unusual plants and trees at Inverleith. Apparently, full-sized trees had been transported from Holyrood to the present site, using a machine invented specially for the job in the eighteen hundreds. Queen Victoria must have found it so charming that she lent her patronage and renamed it the Royal Botanic Gardens, in her honour.

"No. I suppose we will be beneath him when and if he does come back."

"You never know," Grace said in her usual, philosophical way.

CHAPTER 18

Andrew got up in the morning, had a swift breakfast and walked to school, despite there being a bus which could take him almost as far as the school entrance. He loved to stride out, imagining he was a soldier and felt much better for his walk when he reached the old stone building and had to sit for most of the day. Being an extremely bright boy, he usually found that he had finished any task set in the classroom before some children had even started and from this ensued mischief, begat of boredom.

To drop a book on the floor and nip the backside of the girl sitting in front was one of his favourite pastimes, particularly during arithmetic lessons. He loved to see the startled look on the face of the teacher, when Barbara or Gillian leapt up in the air and shrieked out loud and he was famous for his innocent expression when the girl was asked what had happened.

"Come out here, Andrew Donaldson and explain to me what exactly is going on!" would be the cry of Miss Beatty, to which he replied,

"Nothing, Miss. I don't know what you're talking about."

The fact that he had arranged his ruler, so that it stuck into the back of his victim and constantly pushed it out with his thigh while he was being grilled, had something to do with the silence of the girl in question when asked to explain.

The other boys thought he was wonderful and invited him to join them on their weekend adventures many a time but Andrew was never allowed to go.

"Please mother, let me go out with my friends for a couple of hours. I promise to be back for tea. I do feel stupid when I have to say that my mother won't let me come out to play. I feel like an infant You've no idea what it feels like."

Jane did have an idea from another perspective because she had been allowed, in fact encouraged out in the street when she was young. It was a common occurrence for her mother to stand gossiping with other women on the corner, while she and her friends played peevers with a round stone on the pavement or sat in doorways swapping scraps and cardboard dressing dolls. Life had been so easy then. There was no threat of being labelled working-class or being castigated from polite society by joining in the many street games played by her friends. Sometimes now she met women in the village who had been her confidantes when she was a lass and it felt strange and disappointing when they turned away from the woman who lived in the big house at Ecclesmachan; despite the fact that she always, without fail, smiled and greeted them, they rarely answered and sometimes deliberately crossed the road to avoid her. This is not what she wanted for her boys.

So the next time Andrew asked if he could join his pals on Saturday she reluctantly, and nervously because of Michael, said yes. He was given strict instructions to be home by four o'clock and ordered to keep himself tidy, so that his father would have nothing to complain about.

The joy on the face of her child was reward in itself and she cheerfully went off to the garden when she had seen him off the premises. His whistling could be heard for a long time, as he strode down the road in his military fashion.

As soon as he was sure he could not be seen from the house, Andrew rumpled his combed hair, pulled off his tie and put it in his pocket, undoing two buttons at his neck, as he walked. The tie was rolled neatly into a tight ball and thrust into his jacket pocket, which was then flung off and heaved over his shoulder, to be hung from a finger by its neck-loop. This was going to be a grand day. What was it Tammy had said? Can you guddle for trout? Of course he had said yes but now he asked himself what the expression meant. If he had made even a tentative enquiry of his mother, she would have guessed immediately what was planned, so he kept it to himself. The two boys were meeting at the White Gates, which belonged to the mineral railway, and had been used for transporting shale from mine to refinery. As mines were closing, some of the fathers of Andrew's friends had been forced to look for alternative work. This put quite a lot of pressure on the children, unbeknown to their parents, because they were seen as puir wee bairns by the teachers – and word soon got out. A lot of the fights between boys were caused by taunts, such as 'Your da's got no job'.

Andrew had different problems to face and it was only due to his fiendish sense of humour and his capacity for making the other boys laugh that he had been so well accepted. Also, at the slightest hint of a comment about him personally, he was prepared to fight for his honour in any way possible, sticking his fists in the air to prove it.

He reached the main road and crossed over to see his boisterous friend coming out of the sweet shop.

"So she let you out the day, did she?" Tam said, sucking a mint humbug and offering him the paper poke.

"Aye, she did, right enough," he replied. If only his mother and father could hear him now. They would think he was speaking a foreign language. It was always like this. He spoke one way at home and another with his pals. If he didn't do the switch, he would be written off as one of the snobs from Ecclesmachan and that was the worst thing that could have happened to Andrew. He needed friends like birds needed freedom.

"Right then. Let's be off, down to the burn. Come on Andy, follow me," Tam said and started the descent to the thin strip of water in the gully. The way down to the burn had been used by boys for years but this did not make it any easier; another test of manhood. By using the shrubs as points for holding-on, Andrew managed to avoid any cries of 'sissy boy' and arrived at the bottom wearing a big smile. He soon found out that this was not an acceptable facial expression to his cohort and changed it into a grimace while he picked his teeth noisily.

"How many d'you think I'll guddle today, Andy?" Big Tam said.

"I d'know Tam. Maybe one or two."

"One or two! You are fooling aren't you? I c'd find that many in my bath."

He started to laugh and Andrew looked down at the ground.

"G'won, you havenae guddled before have you? There's no shame in admitting it."

He looked up into the bright blue eyes of his leader and decided to come clean, even making a joke out of it, to put himself more at ease.

"OK man, I confess. I don't even know what the bloody word means."

Because he had used a forbidden swear-word, Tam laughed and rolled about on the ground, while this unbelievable fact sank in. There were a few more bloodies and buggers and then they settled down to discuss the intricacies of guddling for trout and anything else that happened to be in the burn. Once it had been decided who would stand upstream and who next, Andrew knew exactly what he was doing and was convinced that he could tickle the belly of a fish as well as the next boy. He was given a position downstream from Tam, so that the more proficient boy could watch the fish moving against the current hoping for flies and his first guddling experience began.

It was amazing how easy it was and Andrew proved he could flick a fish out of the water within half an hour. Then they decided to lie on the bank and guddle the fish in the pools because it was a lot easier to keep perfectly still and let their hands drift with the little current there was. It was a strange experience, tickling the underside of a fish; they were colder than he had imagined and did not seem to notice the movement of his fingers. Sometimes a fish would slide back down into the water with a loud splash, after being flicked onto the bank and, because it had been disturbed, it swam away rapidly. By the time they tired of the occupation, he had done another and he turned onto his back, luxuriating in the bliss of success. Then he suddenly remembered how long they had been in the water. After asking Tam casually and realising they had no means of telling the time, the older boy said,

"Can you see up the brae. There's a few miners walking down. That means the shift's over and it's after four o'clock."

"Oh no! I'm late. I promised to be back by four." He gathered together his belongings and started to slip and slide his way up to the road. As he left, he could hear Tammy muttering, in his gruff tones,

"I know it's not your ma you're worried about, it's your da. Isn't that right?" so he turned and gave him a smile, saying,

"Yep, he's a right b...."

CHAPTER 19

Andrew's first guddle was his last. Flying into the house, over half-an-hour late, he bumped into his father, who had come back early.

"Slow down boy. Who's chasing you?" he said, quite amicably and then he took a closer look at the missile that had hit him. "Good Lord, Andrew. Where did you learn to walk around like that?"

Andrew thought it was his speed and the fact that he had collided with his father that elicited this comment, so he started saying, "I'm sorry, Father. I didn't mean to crash into you. I was rushing to see Mother."

"I expect you were. You look very similar to your mother when she's been planting a tree, only much worse. Take a look at yourself, boy."

When he looked down and saw his filthy front, his mud-encrusted knees and his socks which had disappeared into his grimy shoes, the only thing which kept him from bursting into tears was the thought that he had forgotten his jacket. This further problem filled up his mind, so that he hardly even heard what his father was saying. Then Jane, hearing the shouting, came round the corner and stared in disbelief. She put her hand to her mouth and her eyes seemed to grow in size, as she wondered what punishment would be meted out for this offence. When she had given her permission for him to meet his friends in the village, she had never anticipated this. He must have been rolling in the mud up at the farm to come home looking like that. All she hoped was that he had enjoyed it because he certainly would not enjoy what was going to happen to him now. She could almost see the cogs in Michael's mind moving round, as he thought up a suitable punishment; he was so quiet that it would have to be dreadful. When he spoke, it was as though he were sentencing Andrew to death.

"You can't have become so filthy alone, young man. Please tell me who were your companions in this charade."

She could tell Andrew was loathe to mention the names of any of his friends, in case his father caused more trouble for them, so she jumped in herself.

"I allowed him to meet some boys from school, Michael. It was all my fault. I shouldn't have let him go. Why don't you let him clean himself up and we can talk about it?"

"Your fault! Your fault! I don't think even you could be so stupid as to cover the boy in muck and grass deliberately. This is all his own fault but I have my ways of sorting out such peasantry. I believe you have a holiday at the end of the week, called The Tattie-Picking break. Well, consider yourself broken, my fine young tattie because you will not see that particular schoolyard ever again. I shall spend my own valuable time searching for a place for you at one of the splendid Merchant Schools in Edinburgh, where the boys don't go in for tramping about in the mud at weekends. Subject closed" and he walked off to his sitting room.

"Oh, Mother! He doesn't mean it does he? I can't go to one of those snobbish establishments in the city. I'm an Uphall boy, not a city gent."

"Andrew, you're an Ecclesmachan boy and I hope you are a gent. of some kind. I will have a word with your father and find out exactly what he intends to do but, if I were you, I would remain silent and be thankful that he didn't beat you senseless."

That is exactly how Jane felt herself – thankful. The way Michael had behaved, she was sure he was planning to administer some corporal punishment at least and for him simply to mention another school was totally out of character.

Andrew trudged out to the back door, to remove the offending shoes and thought again about the missing jacket and his tie. There was no way he would be able to retrieve it before tomorrow and if it rained overnight it would be turned into a soggy, muddy pile of navy-blue material. He must get it back sometime and that would mean lying to his mother. At least neither of his parents knew he had met Tam, the butcher's son, to go guddling in the burn and he had been brave enough not to mention his name.

Jane allowed her husband to calm down and then approached him with a glass of whisky, hoping to pour this on the troubled waters and find out what he did intend to do.

"Don't think you can make me forget what your precious baby has done this time," he said when she came into the warm room and put down the glass on his leather-centred desk.

"I merely wondered how I should handle the matter. You obviously didn't have time to think up a punishment on the spot but I think he should have some pleasure removed for turning up looking like a scarecrow."

CHAPTER 20

Michael started to laugh and it was not just a titter or even a guffaw, he started to bellow and snort, to heave and split his sides, making tears run down his reddened face. Then, pulling out a handkerchief and blowing his nose, he became totally serious and, leaning on his arms and peering forward, said,

"My dear wife. I was absolutely serious. The worst possible punishment anyone could devise for that child is to take him away from his low, working class chums and put him in a school for gentlemen – a place he should have been since the age of five and a place I choose, for a change. As for your precious older son, he will go as well. Alright, it will cost me money but the result of my expenditure will be two people who know how to comport themselves, not a couple of country bumpkins. Now do you understand?"

"Oh, Michael. Please don't cut them off from all their friends. You know how much Andrew values his companions and, as for Henry, he is much too reticent to move schools at present. He needs sympathetic surroundings until he is a little older."

"Nonsense. Some men I know send their children off to boarding school when they're six years old. They learn how to behave, away from their doting mamas."

"You don't intend to put them into a boarding school, do you Michael?"

"You make it sound like a home for the bewildered. I assure you that I would, as you say, put them into a boarding school if I wished but the truth is I don't intend to spend that amount of money – not yet anyway. They will be day pupils and come home every day."

"But the travelling – it's far too much for children, after a full day at school."

"Andrew should have thought of that before he joined in with the farmers' boys. Now, I've had enough of this extremely boring conversation. Leave me alone with my cigar for a while, my dear."

Jane left the room, thinking how middle-class Michael had become recently. He wanted nothing to do with the people who worked the land or provided the food for his table, nor did he want to admit to their existence. He was a snob.

000

All seemed to have gone quiet in the house. Not another word had been said to Andrew about his punishment and his father had left home in the middle of the morning, leaving mother to cook lunch. Henry was intrigued to hear that his father planned to move them to a private school in the city and rather looked forward to it. He had been unsuccessful in making friends at primary school, finding them as rough and sarcastic as they found him weak and boring. An all-boys upper-class school might suit him better. They had been discussing the move in Andrew's bedroom at the front of the house, when Henry spotted a rough-looking boy, with brown hair cut in the 'pudding basin' style of the lower orders, walking hesitantly up the drive.

"Hey, Andrew. Isn't that a fellow from your class? He appears to be searching for something or someone – maybe you. Have you taken to inviting them home now?"

Andrew looked out of the window and saw that it was Tam and he was toting a brown carrier bag, which he held behind him.

"I won't be a minute, Henry," he said, as he left the room and bounded downstairs. He fumbled with the catch on the front door and rushed out onto the gravel.

"What are you doing here, Tam?" he asked.

"Why, am I not welcome at your posh house, then?"

"No. I didn't mean it that way. It's just that I got a terrible row for coming home all messed up – and I was almost tortured to tell them who I was with yesterday – and now you turn up! I would rather you hadn't – or they'll know who I was out with and who helped me get into such a mess!"

"I dare say you don't want this back either," he said, thrusting out the carrier bag.

Andrew peered inside, to see his jacket folded up and perfectly clean and dry.

"I found it after you ran off and decided to ask my ma to give it a wee brushing but if you don't want it I can always use it for a working coat when I help my da in the shop."

"Oh, thanks Tam. I was just wondering what I could say to get me out of this prison, to go and find it. I thought, as it rained last night, it would be like an old rag now. Thanks a lot, Tammy."

"Don't go on about it. I just thought it would save you from a bit of trouble, if he found out. I take it you've had your arse lashed?"

"No. That's what's so strange. He didnae touch me. The only thing he did was to go dead quiet and threaten me with a change of school – to a posh place in Edinburgh, no less. But it won't be that easy and I reckon he'll forget all about it, 'specially when he finds out it'll cost him money."

"I wouldn't have thought that was much of a problem, seeing this emporium where you live. You could put half a dozen of my house in there."

The two boys walked backwards a few steps, looking up at the house and Andrew saw Henry peering down at them.

"I think you'd better make yourself scarce, pal," he said and they turned round together and jogged off down the drive. At the gate, Andrew patted Tam on his shoulder and said,

"Thanks again, Tam. You don't know how much this means to me."

"OK lad. We're pals aren't we," he said and wandered off down the road towards Uphall.

CHAPTER 21

The briefcase lay on the floor in the bedroom. This was unusual in itself because Michael only let it out of his sight when he placed it carefully under his desk in the small sitting room he had commandeered for his study. He had left strict instructions with Jane that his papers were never to be disturbed and that the room was only to be cleaned when he was at the office. Although she felt like the hired help, she agreed with his rules, simply because she would rather avoid him than start another fight over anything as ridiculous as his work correspondence.

However, the presence of the briefcase on the bedroom floor, when he was out with his colleagues that Saturday morning, was sufficiently unusual to tempt her into some underhand behaviour. She closed the door surreptitiously, not knowing why, and picked up the black leather bag. There was a lock in the middle but it had been left unfastened, so all she had to do to examine the inside was to pull up the flap. The reason for this subterfuge was beyond her and the stupid action was totally uncharacteristic but she flung the rough leather top of the briefcase back.

There, inside, was the usual collection of foolscap papers that normally littered the oblong surface of Michael's desk but right at the back, down in the depths, was a small, cream letter. She tentatively took hold of it by the corner and pulled it towards her. Michael's name and office address were written in mauve ink, in a fine, loopy hand, the writing of a woman.

Perhaps it was the wife of one of his managers, writing to thank him for some kindness to her husband. Perhaps it was the mother of an apprentice, writing for her son. Perhaps, it was a personal letter – too personal to be sent to his home address, to risk it being opened by his wife.

With shaking hands, she withdrew the two pages of cream, heavily textured notepaper and read,

My dearest Michael,

I have been in seventh heaven since we talked last weekend and I know you will not object to this correspondence at your place of work, to tell you how much I am starting to love you.
    The letter went on in similar vein for two full pages and finished by saying, *You know you have all my love, Enid.* Jane sat on the bed she shared with her unfaithful husband, holding the proof of his infidelity, wanting to tear it into small pieces of confetti and sprinkle it all over his pillow. Her mind would not accept the fact at first. She thought of all the times she had longed for some token of affection; how she had buried her own longings in hard work, purely to avoid being thought of as coarse and unfeminine when the man she had married had been committing adultery behind her back. It was possible that work colleagues knew about this liaison and were laughing at her gullibility; no wonder he refused to invite people from work to come to the house for dinner or introduce her to any of the wives who could call on her for afternoon tea.
    Quite suddenly, she burst into tears; but she was still sensible enough to realise that the letter was still in her hands and in danger of being washed away in the flood, so she carefully folded it and replaced it in the case, carefully fastening each strap. Her sobbing turned into hysterical yelping and loud moaning, until she realised that it was almost time for her boys to return from their music class. Sniffing and taking huge breaths, she straightened the counterpane and turned over the pillow on which she had cried, then went to the wardrobe mirror and pulled her clothing back into some semblance of orderliness. Even the front of her dress felt damp but it would soon dry. Her sons must never see her in this state.
    She went downstairs, made herself some tea and sat at the kitchen table, wondering why she had been so upset. After all, she did not love this man and he obviously did not care for her, not in the slightest. She had wept from pride, nothing else. She did not want anyone to think she was a lesser mortal than her husband. How often had he taken her in his arms and said that he loved her? None. How many times, during their marriage of over ten years? How regularly had he taken her out to hotels or restaurants, to meet his fine friends, including no doubt his

woman friend? She could count the occasions on the fingers of one hand.

After suffering so much deprecation at his hands and now discovering his true worth, she went from monumental sadness to tremendous joy. She had no need to fear him or to respect him for his social position ever again. The tables had been truly turned and she held the secret of her own future in her faultless memory, which enabled her to remember every single word of the sad, little missive she had found in Michael's possession. She even knew the first name and address of the ridiculous woman who had the temerity to try to steal away her husband. Now she knew what future action she must take.

When Michael returned from his supposed meeting with colleagues, there was no trace of change in Jane whatsoever. Her manner was exactly as it usually was – efficient and kindly. Her boys had found her making cakes and scones when they returned, filling the kitchen with the warm, vanilla scents of baking straight from the oven and she had taken time to listen to their violin and piano pieces and to applaud when they had finished; everything a good mother would do. Michael had asked whether they had attended their classes, nodded and then disappeared, to collect his forgotten briefcase and then to shut himself into his study. Jane imagined him writing a response to his soppy love letter and wondered if she should open the door and make him spray blots onto the page in his feverish attempts to conceal it; but was this man worth the effort?

000

Over the next weeks, she found out by stealth the surname of Enid and the whereabouts of the spare key to Michael's briefcase. This meant that she had all the ammunition she required, when she required it, which was not at the present time. Her life had become bearable because she knew she was in charge and, as a result, she became relaxed and even cheerful.

When the boys were given a place at George Heriot's School on the south side of Edinburgh and arrangements were made for them to travel to the splendid stone edifice for, as Michael described it, 'a proper education', she merely accepted it and bought their uniforms. To her, it was coincidental that the school had been changed from a hospital endowed by an Edinburgh jeweller, Jinglin' Geordie Heriot, and once used by Oliver Cromwell for his injured troops, into a place of education in the past for 'puir fatherless bairns'. Amazingly, her own poor, almost-fatherless, boys took this change in their fortunes in their stride and seemed to fit in to the classes to which they were allotted with the minimum of fuss. No doubt Henry had talked seriously to his brother to accomplish this change of attitude for Andrew.

Jane had no idea how much Andrew missed his schoolmates, nor how he spent hours lying in bed, wondering how he could continue to see his new but neglected friend, Tam.

000

Rob had been taken on at the Botanics, with the proviso that his employment would be reviewed at Christmas. As that time approached and he appeared to be settling in extremely well, the Head Gardener was prepared to offer him a permanent position and called him into his office to discuss the terms.

"Now Rob. You seem to have approached your job with a definite amount of professionalism, so much so that I feel you would make a good hot-house man. I know I can trust you with delicate plants and their maintenance, so what do you say?"

Over the last few weeks, Rob had gone over this very scene in his mind and had almost come to the conclusion that he would sell up his cottage and move to the outskirts of Edinburgh, so that he could pursue this new career. He was fascinated by tropical plants and those new additions to the Palm House brought back from China recently by Mr George Forrest and he had even had the honour of helping to unpack the precious finds, along with the boss of the glasshouse. Forrest had made several expeditions to collect cuttings, seeds and even fully grown plants for the Botanic Gardens and he was a visionary when it came to stocking the protected areas of a collection in a cold country with plants from an opposite climate. He looked just like an ordinary gardener, in his collarless white shirt, his rough jacket and trilby hat and yet he had travelled to the far ends of the Earth to search for unusual samples for this lucky garden in Edinburgh. While the work was going on, Rob had gazed at the glass ceiling of the tallest palm house in Britain and thought how lucky he was to be involved in such a rare project. Yet, a certain part of him wanted to be out in the open, away from the heat which was necessary for the survival of the palms. How he loved the feel of the wind in his face and the earth in his hands, as he sieved the fine tilth of soil through his fingers. Cold and wet never worried him; in fact he wallowed in the changing seasons, accepting that winter followed the tapestry of colour in autumn but that spring and summer were never far away, even when black ice made it impossible to walk.

"Well lad, what do you say? Have I taken on a new hot-house gardener or not? I know old Bill would be glad of your help."

Rob smiled down into his collar. "When I came in here this morning, I was all prepared to accept whatever you had to offer but I have to say that I'm going to turn you down, Jock. The thought of the great outdoors and the changing seasons just came into my head and I have to ask if you can give me a different job – something where I can battle with the elements, not hide from the wind and the rain."

"Well I'm sorry, young Rob. There's nothing else going in the main gardens. You know yourself how these jobs are sought after and I have a waiting list as long as my arm for the outside sections. Won't you change your mind. We don't want to lose you lad?"

"I can't, Jock. I must be outside or I'll wither and die – just as your palm trees would if they were put in the wrong conditions. If you can't give me an outside job, I'm afraid I must depart."

"There's nothing for it then, son. I can't offer you anything else, not yet at any rate. Keep in touch though and I'll see what I can do in the future. It looks as if you'll be leaving at Christmas then…"

"Aye."

"I'll miss you, man, whenever I hear that word," he said, with a sad little smile on his weather-beaten face.

CHAPTER 22

Christmas Day dawned fine and clear, although the ground was covered in ice and it was hard work attempting to reach the compost heap. Jane kept every morsel of biodegradable waste to add to the heavy soil in her garden, hoping to lighten it as well as feed the plants with nutritious vegetation from the kitchen.

As she made her way tentatively towards the pair of collecting boxes, roughly but capably made from wood and chicken wire by Rob, she slid and slipped even on the gravel and several times her bucket full of apple and carrot peelings and outer leaves from the Brussels sprouts almost left her hand. What if her stockings were laddered; that would be another job, or another explanation to Michael that she had ,to buy some new ones. At last she reached the growing mass of foliage and grass clippings, which she had covered with a piece of old carpet found in the loft. She deposited the contents of her bucket underneath it then stood for a while, looking around the winter garden, eyeing up the stalks of dormant perennials, when there was a rustling at foot level and a lone, male blackbird bravely popped out. He tipped his head on one side and seemed to stare at her, almost asking for some scraps for himself, so she broke a piece of crusty bread, from her pocket, into crumbs and threw it down. Immediately, he moved forward on his stick-like legs and grabbed a small piece, hurrying back into the undergrowth to demolish it.

Jane remembered how Rob would toss the remains of his lunchtime piece onto the ground for the birds and how he always said he planted three seeds instead of one, so there was one for the birds, one for the wind and one to grow. She wondered what kind of a Christmas he was having in Edinburgh, alone.

The preparations for the Christmas dinner were almost done and she thought how wonderful it would have been if she had had a daughter to help her. Boys only took an interest in food once it was cooked and on a plate in front of them; girls also enjoyed the creative business of cooking it.

She had not seen Michael all morning; not since the ceremonial opening of presents around the tree. They had gathered together at eleven o'clock this morning, dressed in their finery, and he had put himself in charge of handing out the gifts. No-one was allowed to touch their package until the others were fully attentive. And when all had admired it, the next one was handed out. Her present from Michael had been Mrs Beeton's book of Household Management and hers to him was a gold tie-pin. The boys received games, as well as their full Christmas stockings which had been hung at the fireplace in true tradition and had been filled by her with apples and oranges, chocolate bars, drawing paper and crayons, handkerchiefs and new toothbrushes, collected over the months with her food shopping and from the newsagents.

As soon as the distribution of presents was over, Jane took the pile of used wrapping paper away to the kitchen and left the men to their games. Lunch was soon assembled and there was laughter and happiness in the candlelit dining room that afternoon. Michael appeared imperturbable after his several glasses of whisky and then wine, so the boys made the most of his mood and joked with each other right under his nose. If it were possible to bottle the contents of a day, this is the one Jane would conserve. The family felt like a real family and no brusque words were spoken. Perhaps everything would come right after all. Perhaps her imagination had run away with her and there was no more to Michael's ill-temper than problems at work.. Perhaps she would have the courage to bring up the subject while he was in such a pleasant frame of mind.

After she had cleared away the dirty dishes and washed them in the large white sink, she carefully wiped the silver cutlery which was used for special occasions. As she pushed the end of a drying up cloth between the tines of a fork, a picture of old Grace came into her head, sitting all alone with her little cat for company. She finished the work and went into the sitting room, where Michael was reading. Andrew had just finished a game of draughts with his brother and was putting the little wooden counters into the box provided.

"If you are all happy, I thought I would go next door, to wish Grace a Merry Christmas. I have made up a parcel of cake and biscuits, as well as the spare cracker from the dinner table. I know for a fact that she is spending the festive season by herself, as usual."

"You can't stop yourself from being Mrs Busybody, can you?" Michael said, raising his eyes from his magazine and grinning sarcastically. "Or is it Mrs Magnanimous because you're the mistress of the big house?"

"Neither. I just feel sorry for an old lady who has no company at this time of year. I will be back to make your tea."

"Mother, wait for me and I will come with you," said Andrew confidently, casting a quick glance at his father, who had gone back to his reading and was now ignoring everyone.

"I hope you don't mind but I want to read my book," Henry said.

"No dear, that's quite alright. Are you sure you want to come, Andrew. It will just be gossiping with Mrs Sanderson?"

"Yes, I do. I like her little cat."

Jane knew this was an excuse for his sensitivity, so she held out her hand and pulled him to his feet, smiling fondly at Henry as they went out the door.

000

The bell rang in the hall of the house next door and Jane heard the shuffling, beslippered footsteps of her old neighbour, as she came to open the large front door. Her surprise was multiplied when she saw that Andrew stood beside his mother.

"Oh, my dears, how good to see you. What can I do for you? Is there a problem?"

"No, Grace, no problem. We have come to wish you a Happy Christmas and hope you can spare some time for two waifs and strays who find themselves on your doorstep."

"But of course. Come along in, both of you. How on earth did you manage to walk on the ice. I went out with some crumbs for the birdies and had to gather all my strength to get back in again – it's so slippery!"

"You shouldn't have gone out at all, Grace. You could have landed on your back in this weather."

"I couldn't leave my wee feathered friends with nothing to eat on Christmas Day, now, could I?"

Jane made a mental note to feed her own feathered friends every day from now on. Grace was quite right – they needed some nourishment now all the berries had gone.

The old lady led the way into her sitting room, where the fire was blazing up the chimney and the sleek, fluffy cat lay on the chair Grace had just vacated. It looked up at the unusual entrance of visitors to her domain, then let her chin fall back onto her front paws, luxuriating in the heat of the fire and the soft, folded rug on the chair.

"Oh, isn't she lovely," said Andrew and went forward to pat the head of the little companion.

"Yes. I think she enjoys being an only child, now that her brother has gone to Jesus. She gets all the fuss and all the little treats now. Do you know, young man, she ate a whole chicken breast for her Christmas Dinner – almost as much as me! What a greedy little pussy – but it is Christmas Day."

Andrew smiled understandingly and stood back so that Grace could take up her place once more.

"Thank you my dear. Which one are you? I always forget names these days. I know there's a Henry and an Andrew but I'm ashamed to say that I don't know one from the other."

"I'm Andrew. My brother's older than me and he's called Henry."

"That's good, Andrew. Now I shall never forget you again. Andrew is the one who came to see me and pussy on Christmas Day. Now, I will get you some tea and goodies. Just you two wait there and I won't be long in the kitchen."

"Before you dash off, Grace, here's a little Christmas treat for you. It's just some Christmas cake and home-made items and a cracker from the table."

"Ooh, a cracker! I haven't had one for years. Come along and pull it with me, my boy," she said and they heaved at either end, until a motto and a toy mouse fell out. The motto was read instantly and the tiny mouse given to little Lucy as a Christmas present.

"Let me give you a hand," said Jane, moving to the door.

"No, indeed. You have been cooking all morning, my dear. Let me get you a little treat for being such a good neighbour. I've been here for more years than I care to remember and nobody has ever rung my bell on Christmas Day and that, despite the fact that I always buy plenty of Christmas food for visitors, just in case."

Jane had not the heart to explain how full she felt and how she had even planned to miss her own tea back at home. Instead she thanked Grace profusely and, while she was out, admonished Andrew to accept anything he was offered.

"You see, darling. Grace doesn't have a Christmas Day as we do and our coming to call is very exciting for her. Just making up a tea tray on this special day will remain in her memory forever."

"I know mother. She never has visitors, does she? Every time she sees us on the wall – me and Henry – she rushes out with juice and biscuits. We never say no thank you because we would hate to hurt her feelings – and sometimes the birds get the biscuits, if we've just had some at home. She's a nice person. I like her a lot."

Grace came bustling back with a laden tray of cakes and biscuits and asked Andrew if he would help with another tray of china while she brought the teapot. Jane wondered if she should offer to do it instead, knowing how clumsy Andrew could be but, when she saw him puff out his chest and say,

"Of course, Mrs Sanderson. Of course I will," she could not spoil his moment of glory and just sat with her fingers crossed under the coffee table.

He managed extremely well and Jane could see him measuring his steps through the doorway and over the threadbare oriental rug. When he reached the low table, he allowed his breath to come out and, after putting down the heavy tray, he sat down opposite Jane on the settee, a wide smile on his face.

Pieces of gossip and pieces of cake were handed round and Andrew was allowed to nurse the friendly cat on his knee until they finished and took their leave. As they left the house, Grace said,

"I hope this won't be the last time you come in for a cup of tea and a chat, my dear. Let's make this the first of many. I would like that." She would have to remember that invitation, as the lovely old lady had really enjoyed their visit.

Jane and Andrew walked carefully back home and, on the way, Andrew distributed pieces of ginger cake, chocolate cake, iced buns and cream biscuits all over the borders – well out of sight of the house next door.

"Your pockets must have been full but thank you for accepting all that. It meant a lot to her."

"I know. Henry showed me how to do that. He does it all the time, even at home."

Now she knew. Michael was always encouraging Henry to eat plenty at mealtimes, even too much, and this is how he got around it.

They arrived back and Jane made a delicious tea of Christmas cake, mince pies and chocolate-covered biscuits, all of which she personally did without. She noticed that Andrew had regained his appetite and tucked-in with his father and brother, then they all relaxed in easy chairs until it became really dark outside. The room was lit by the tiny candles on the Christmas tree and Jane noticed that Michael had dropped off to sleep. This had been a truly wonderful day.

That night, when she and Michael drifted upstairs to their bedroom, they walked sleepily together and smiled at each other at the turn of the stairs – something they had not done since they were first married. Although Jane was exhausted from her busy day, she was also contented because all had gone so well and because the whole family appeared to be happy, particularly Michael. He had never lost his good looks and, even though he was slim but of an unathletic build, he remained attractive in an academic way. He must have passed on his dark hair and heavy eyebrows to Henry but the boy was more like her father, in build, with his tall frame. Michael's habit of always dressing in an ultra-tidy way, nearing perfection, had pleased her in their early days and it was good to know that he was such a clean, meticulous person as far as hygiene was concerned, even though he could be somewhat obsessive.

They went into the spacious bedroom and put on the light, Michael rushing across to draw the curtains, although there was nothing but hills to see from the front of the house. He took off his clothing, folding each piece carefully and putting it on the slipper chair in the window. Then, standing in front of the wardrobe mirror, he held in his stomach and admired his profile. All this time, Jane was fussing over her own undergarments and running down her silk stockings, which she rolled into a ball for the following day but she glanced up at her husband from time to time, amused at his unusual actions. When she had put her sensible pink flannelette nightdress over her head and smoothed it into place, she allowed herself a full look at the man on the other side of the bed. He took his pyjamas from their usual place under the stone hot water bottle she had placed there earlier. When she was comfortably settled under the blankets, he took her in his arms and made love to her, for the first time in months. And he caressed her, as he used to do in the early days of their marriage. What a wonderful surprise.

But she spent Hogmanay alone by the fire because Michael had gone out with some friends; drinking a solitary toast in sherry to absent friends, before she went to bed. The bells of the local church rang out the chimes for midnight, as she did so. She slipped further down under the blankets and closed her eyes, visualizing Rob, before she made the most important New Year's Resolution of her life.

I will remain totally faithful to the man I have married, regardless of his behaviour, for the sake of my children and the vows I took all those years ago.

And long before it was one o'clock in the year of 1930, she was fast asleep.

CHAPTER 23

That spring was full of the pleasure of her garden and the joy of having a dear old friend, who never judged and never harkened back to the past. Grace's mind was consistently fixed on the next bit of interest, be it a meeting of the Scottish WI in the church hall or a walk into the village to buy dress material, which she made up on her old Singer sewing machine whilst watching the hills from her window upstairs. Jane had taken to helping Grace in her shopping and in the house, which was far too big for one lone person, even though a woman from the village came in to clean every week.

One rainy day, Grace invited Jane to go up to her 'maid's room' at the back of the house and showed her the dozens of crocheted and hand-stitched linen doilies, christening gowns and nightdress cases her mother and grandmother had made.

"I want to clear out this room. These bits and pieces have been lying around for too long. I wondered if you would be a dear and help me?"

Of course Jane agreed and the sorting out of bundles of beautifully-sewn items led to Grace expounding on her family history. Her father had been a seaman, who had gone off in his ship and never returned. His sea chest, which was now the container for her collection of sewn items, had returned without him. Not long afterwards, her mother had died, as Grace said of a broken heart and the little girl had been brought up by her grandmother in the very house they were in now. She had been educated at a Dame's School in Edinburgh, where her reading, writing and arithmetic were supplemented with fine sewing, tapestry and cooking. She was also taught how to use a typewriter and, after staying on to teach, she took employment with a lawyer in Edinburgh. The man was her senior by many years and had an invalid wife, who subsequently died, leaving one daughter.

All through the wife's illness and at the time of her death, Grace had handled many formalities of a personal nature, including the funeral arrangements, with the result that her employer asked her to walk out with him, after a suitable period of mourning. But the daughter was furious and vowed never to speak to her father again. However, he proposed marriage to Grace, making it very clear that he was only looking for companionship and she accepted because he was the father-figure she had been searching for all these years, with the result that she remained childless. At first, he had tried to persuade her to move into his large house in Trinity, Edinburgh but she had refused, saying she was happy in her grandmother's house and would rather stay there. Realising that it was the house or him, he agreed to move in with her at Ecclesmachan, with the proviso that any of his possessions were passed on to his daughter at his death. For a while their house was like an antiques warehouse but gradually they sold or gave away many pieces and, Grace said with a smirk, much of what could be seen now had belonged to her own family. She had put his furniture into a spare room and, when he died, it was passed on to his daughter and was never missed.

Now it was a case of parting with the trivia of life, because she worried that her husband's daughter would come along when she died and throw out everything she had loved for so long – as she had no family of her own. She had not mentioned it in so many words but the reason she wanted Jane's help was because she saw in her a soulmate, who might possibly take some of her beloved pieces and care for them.

Not knowing anything about this, Jane expounded on the complicated workmanship and delightful styling of the vast numbers of sewn articles, so much so that Grace decided to play her trump card.

"Would you like some of them, dear?"

"Oh I couldn't be so presumptuous, Grace."

"But, can't you see, I have no daughter who could take them and when I have gone they could well be put in the dustbin."

"What about your stepdaughter? Surely she would…"

"No. I know for certain that she would be the one to throw them out."

Jane was very sad for her dear old friend and said, "In that case, I accept, with many, many thanks. I never thought I would be so lucky and I assure you I will treasure them, as you have."

Grace was happy once more and the tidying out of the maid's room continued, until all was cleared and Jane stood in the doorway, bearing a huge bundle of assorted pieces of sewing. Then came the big surprise.

"You have been so kind, Jane, but I find I must ask of you one more favour. Would you have room in your house for the sea chest?"

Jane was aghast. For Grace to hand over the trunk that had belonged to her own dead father was too much. How could she part with such a nostalgic part of her life? She opened her mouth to say so and then, seeing the apprehensive look on her face, decided not to upset her old friend any more and, instead, just said,

"I would be delighted and honoured to have it, Grace. When my boys come home from school I will ask them to come with me and collect it."

000

The sea chest was left in the laundry room until Michael came home from work. He took one look at it and said,

"What's that piece of junk in the laundry room? Put it round the back of the garage or get someone to shift it. I know just the man."

CHAPTER 24

Rather than argue, Jane agreed to remove it from the house and planned where to put it the following day. The old sea chest, which had survived since the early nineteenth century, was not going to be carted away by someone who worked for Michael. She could see that the rough oak of its exterior and the naïve painting of the interior would not fit in with the dark mahogany furniture of their main rooms but she had hoped it could be used in a guest bedroom or a working area of the house. However, what Michael said was important and she knew exactly where she would put it. At the bottom of the garden was an out-house, more a potting shed which had been used as a summerhouse by the previous owner. Jane had thought about decorating it inside and using it as a secret place where she could go to think in solitude. It could hardly be seen from the house because branches of trees had grown over the roof and honeysuckle clung to its sides, so that the only evidence of it was the glass doors and adjacent windows, looking out to the south and away from the house.

This was where she trundled the sea chest the following day, on its small wheels, heaving it along then making it take large steps by turning it round in circles, until she eventually reached the shed with the heavy object. If she had asked Michael to help her move it, she knew what his reaction would have been, so rather than lose Grace's treasured sea chest, she struggled with it herself. Once in the summerhouse, she sat down on the top surface and tried to imagine a sailor doing the same thing, thinking of his family at home and wondering when he would see them again. She had similar thoughts, but not about her family.

The placing of the trunk encouraged Jane to clean out the little room and when she had finished, the place shone from stained ceiling to pine floorboards and the chest took pride of place under the window, which she planned to dress with some gingham curtains from her new pile of sewing fabrics. There was a long cushion, which they had taken away from a window embrasure which would make a comfortable seat for the chest and it could also be covered in the same blue gingham. She would bring Grace down to see what she had done with her father's chest. And she would elaborate on how she would decorate the garden shed, to make it into a workroom for herself, away from the rest of the family; Grace would appreciate that.

000

Rob moved back into his small cottage in Uphall. Nothing had really changed in the time he had spent at the Botanics and he was glad he had taken the trouble to clean it when he left and check on it from time to time. Housework was not his idea of a manly occupation but a little tidying and dusting was seen by him to be a necessity if the house was left empty. Now he was back home he would revert to his usual routine of a weekly clean-up and turnout of old newspapers and compost rubbish.

He made his way along to the grocers for the purchase of basic items, thinking how good it would be to eat alone. He had enjoyed the company of his cousin, Alistair, for a time and then, preferring solitude, had begun to resent his constant presence, particularly during meal times.

"Hello, my friend," said Mr Robertson. "I thought you'd left the country. I havenae seen you for a long time."

"Aye, I've been working in Edinburgh but that's all over now. I'm back to pick up where I left off. All I hope is I haven't lost all my customers."

"I can assure you that a lot of folk'll be glad to see you back, Rob. The number of my regulars who've asked about you…"

"Have you seen Mrs Sanderson?"

"I have that. She's got that young neighbour of hers helping in the garden, since you left. She's an energetic soul, that Mrs Donaldson and she's got the same amount of her own garden to do as well."

"Well, maybe I'll call and see if she wants me back – that'll give the young lass a bit of a break."

After picking up his carrier bag full of sugar, butter, milk and other bits and pieces, Rob left the shop and wondered when he should start on his rounds. It was a bit cheeky, leaving his clients and then expecting to regain them but they were all pleasant souls and perhaps they would understand. He decided to wait until Monday morning.

000

Now she had a place where she could hide, Jane felt better about life. She loved her big house but there was nowhere she could call her own, despite the many rooms, so the summerhouse became her bolt-hole, the way his study was Michael's. She had decided to restart her journal. All through her teenage years, when she had private problems she would write them in her diary, finding this cathartic exercise good for her mental well-being, seeing the book as an invisible friend, like children sometimes have when they're young and lonely. And, after her marriage, she had kept her diary hidden in her underwear drawer. But she always worried it would be found. Not having a husband who cared two jots for her daily difficulties and having no female friend with whom to share her secrets, the journal took their place. And it was very important to her.

It was doubly necessary to hide her journal because today, she had taken on a cleaner. In fact it was the same woman who came to Grace, and Jane had argued with herself that there was no reason for her to knock herself out with household chores when Michael never noticed a miniscule thing in the house – apart from what was wrong of course. In the past she had rushed around with a broom and carpet sweeper, finishing off with a yellow duster and Michael would bring to her attention a line of dust on the skirting board when he returned home. Now she could blame any omissions on the cleaning lady and put her guilty feelings away forever.

So, while Mrs Morgan swept and polished, Jane wandered down to the summerhouse, lifted the lid of the sea chest, marvelling for the umpteenth time at the brightly-painted inside of the lid. Several trees had been drawn, as if the owner had missed dry land so much that he had to remind himself daily; swirls and curls surrounded a crown with a jewelled top and two flags. One of them was the Scottish cross but she had no idea what the other was; there were horizontal lines and a small square in the top right-hand corner with what looked like a Union Jack – perhaps some naval flag. She lifted the lid of a small compartment at the side and retrieved her journal and pen, then sat on top of the warm, wooden trunk to relate her day.

Next door, Rob was knocking and ringing the doorbell at Grace's house and there was no reply. He knew the old lady never went out now and that her hearing was extremely good, so he was puzzled. After beating on the door a few more times, he decided to walk around to the back of the house to see if there was any activity. He felt bad about peering in at the window of the kitchen but knew it was in a good cause and felt sure Grace would forgive him. There was no sign. He moved along to the living room window and repeated his nosy behaviour. There, on the rag rug, was the prone figure of Grace, her little cat nestled by her side. What could he do?

Looking around him, hoping to find a solution, he caught sight of a flash of light from the garden next door and, moving towards the fence, he noticed the old potting shed had been cleaned and the sun was bouncing off the shiny windows. As he looked, the door opened and out came Jane.

"Jane, Jane!" he called, without a second thought that her husband might be home.

She stared around her disbelievingly, until she caught sight of Rob, who was waving frantically from the next door garden. She ran across to him, to find herself assailed with sentences, rattled off at top speed and eventually she managed to deduce that there was a problem in Grace's living room.

She ran to the foot of her garden, out of the gate and into the next garden, where Rob was standing, fidgeting at the back door.

"Look! She's just lying on the floor, not moving. We must break a window and climb in."

"There's no need for that. I know where she keeps her spare key, in the garage. Hold on and I'll fetch it."

Within minutes they were inside the house and Jane had found a weak pulse in Grace's wrist. She ran at top speed back home and telephoned the doctor, who in turn rang for an ambulance, to take the poor old lady to hospital.

When all the excitement was over, Jane and Rob sat down on a garden seat and took a few deep breaths.

"I just called to see if she wanted me to carry on with the garden, now I'm back home," he said.

"You're back from Edinburgh. For good?"

"I reckon so."

"Why did you come back?"

"I couldn't take the idea of being shut in a glasshouse all day. That's the job they offered me."

"Oh no, I wouldn't like that at all."

"There was one other reason why I had to come back."

"What was that?" she said, breathlessly.

"You."

"Me?" She was delighted to hear this but tried to remain cool.

"I had to see you again. I haven't been able to get you out of my mind, no matter how hard I tried. I know it's wrong but I had to see you again. I couldn't forget that kiss."

"Me neither", she said more calmly than she felt. "But I know there's no future for us."

"Who cares about the future. Can't we just live for the present?"

"I suppose we must. It will be difficult."

"Life's difficult," he smiled, taking her hand in his and they kissed, gently. For Jane that was the most wonderful feeling. She loved this man so much.

CHAPTER 25

"I'm sorry I haven't been to see you until now, Grace," Jane said quietly to the old lady in the hospital ward. All the people around were old ladies, some in beds and some sitting on chairs in their dressing-gowns. Several were wandering aimlessly about in nighties, muttering to themselves. Suddenly, a person with a large purple blotch on her cheek stopped Jane and, grabbing her wrist, said,

"Take it away, mother. You know I hate rice pudding. You see that man in the corner, he's murdered my brother, for money." She was obviously out of her mind.

It was a frightening place to be and she wished fervently that her dear friend was not there. She had heard about old people with dementia but never understood what it was. When she spoke, Jane wished even more that it had been possible to keep Grace at home.

"You haven't been to see me, Lucy," she said, calling Jane by the cat's name. "I wish you had been here last night because all the cats were howling and three dead cats were on my bed in the morning. I had to ask the nurse to take them away."

Obviously, Grace's mind was also affected in some way.

"It's alright Grace. It's me, Jane, your next-door neighbour and friend. I've come to make sure you come home as quickly as possible."

"Good, good. I have to feed my pussy," she said, drifting off to sleep, not knowing that Jane had been feeding Lucy every day.

Jane had heard of people reacting this way to drugs, so she found a nurse and asked her whether Grace had been given any medicine.

"Of course she has. They all have to have tranquilizers in here, to keep them manageable. Apart from that she took a hefty fall and the doctor said she needed something for that."

Feeling extremely worried, Jane said, "I think she has become confused because of the mixture of medicines."

"How would you know! They're all confused here. It's called senile dementia. You must know how old she is."

"Yes, but she was as bright as a button when she came here. I am her neighbour and see her regularly."

"Well, she's not now. Anyway, I have a lot of work to do and must rush."

Jane felt sick to her stomach at this response to the illness of an old person. Nobody deserved such treatment when they were ill and what had happened to that good old-fashioned feeling of respect for one's elders. No doubt the nurses had an extremely tough time, looking after a ward full of people who didn't understand where they were, some worse than others. She did understand that they must lay down some laws for everyone, just to keep themselves sane. She could never be in that position herself, purely because she had too much sympathy for each individual. She simply must get Grace out of this hell-hole as soon as possible. It was how she imagined Dante's Inferno or a scene from a depiction of Hades and she must see what she could do. But she knew that no hospital was the same and she did feel sorry for the nurses who had to cope with such problems daily.

Back at home she put the wheels in motion, partly because she felt she had to, Grace having no living relatives, and because there was a definite unfairness being perpetrated there.

The cleaner, Mrs Morgan, told her of a friend who was happy to care for invalids in their own homes and she was contacted regarding spending some time with Grace because Jane knew there would be a necessity for overnight nursing. She had been putting food out for Lucy at her own back door, hoping the cat would see her as a friend and young Andrew monitored it each day, reporting back to his mother about the quantity eaten; this seemed to work.

When she went back to see Grace, she told her of the plans she had made and saw her visibly improve after hearing it. They even had a normal conversation, during which several old ladies came over to stare and to eavesdrop but Jane did not care. She merely treated them kindly and went on with her chat to Grace, until they became bored and moved off. As a final undertaking she went to the Matron's office and discussed

Grace with her. She was told that it depended on 'doctor's decision after his rounds in the morning' and she went back to Grace and informed her.

"Right," said the weak and weary voice from the iron bed. "I must make a good impression then" and Jane knew she would.

000

Grace came home two days later and Jane was there to greet her. Ten minutes after her removal upstairs from the ambulance, Rob appeared, bearing the biggest bouquet ever and he asked Jane to take it upstairs for him.

"No. I won't do that," she said, mischievously. "Take them up yourself."

"Am I allowed?"

"Yes you're allowed - you sound like Andrew. She is lying in her own bed, with clean sheets and a cup of tea. I know she will be delighted to see you."

He leapt up the stairs, two at a time, his bouquet held carefully in front of him and, before entering the Victorian bedroom, he stopped to smooth down his hair and straighten his clothes, which was his normal gardening garb but much cleaner than usual. As he peeped around the door, Jane heard Grace say, in her brittle but cheerful voice,

"Come in my boy, come in. What a lovely surprise. Are you back for a holiday?"

"No, Mrs Sanderson, I'm back for good. I gave up my job at the Botanics and came back to Uphall."

The sounds upstairs were of gladness and even excitement and Jane knew that this would be the best tonic Grace could ever have, talking about her beloved garden with the man who would keep it in prime condition.

Sadly, Grace deteriorated instead of recovering but Jane and Rob made sure that her mind was at rest, by supervising the house and garden and, more importantly, Lucy. Andrew was delighted to have an animal about and took it upon himself to feed her and brush her – even miaowing to her in a mysterious language, apparently understood by both of them. Henry quietly assisted Rob outdoors but never commented on his exertions, although Rob informed Jane of his industry and said he was becoming a really proficient gardener.

This went on for several seasons, until one day the doctor was called out and informed Jane that he felt the old lady had not long to live.

"Of course she might surprise us and make another phenomenal recovery but I very much doubt it. She is very old and her body is worn out. From my experience of Grace, I would say she has decided to let her batteries run down now. I notice you said that she eats very little and drinks even less and that is a sure sign."

So Grace left this world as happy as a very old lady could be, surrounded by friends, knowing her beloved pussy was being well cared for.

000

All arrangements were made, a small funeral was held in the lovely old local church and Jane returned to her own home, to catch up on the myriad jobs left undone during her stint with Grace. Rob continued with the garden, until told otherwise by the lawyer, so he could be seen trimming and planting now that it was once again Spring and Jane felt contented just knowing he was there.

One day, her doorbell rang and she went to answer it, still wearing her apron from the kitchen. There was a tidy, dumpy little woman on the step, wearing a navy blue worsted coat, a paler blue scarf at her neck and a darker blue hat sitting perfectly horizontally on her head. Her hands were covered in black gloves and her shoes were of the laced-up variety, also in black. Jane had a premonition but had no time to consider it because the person said,

"Good morning. Could you tell your mistress that Miss Sanderson is here to see her. I would appreciate it if you were quick, as I have many things to do."

Jane felt her mouth go into a surprised 'o', before she said,

"I am the mistress of this house. You have caught me at my baking, otherwise you might have realised that." Thinking how rude she sounded, she said, "I'm sorry, I didn't mean to sound so cross. It's just that I'm very busy today."

The woman looked her up and down and said, "So am I, so I would appreciate a few minutes of your valuable time, if that's not asking too much."

Jane decided to be as polite as she could be, in the hopes that it would rub off onto her guest and asked Miss Sanderson to come in. So this was the step-daughter Grace had had to put up with for many years; the woman who had not even bothered to attend Grace's funeral. They went into the sitting room at the front of the house and Jane noticed the woman looking round at her possessions, so she slowly removed her apron and deliberately placed it on the back of one of the antique chairs.

"Can I get you some tea or perhaps coffee?" she asked.

"No thank you. I must hurry. I have the lawyer to see today."

They sat down opposite each other in two fireside chairs, Jane very aware that the fire was not lit until the evening but her visitor had obviously decided to keep her coat on because she pulled it closely around her, once settled. She played with the handle and catch of her black leather handbag as she talked.

"The reason I am here is to ask you what has happened to many pictures and some furniture, which I know were in the house next door the last time I visited."

Jane wondered how she could possibly have remembered that, as she hadn't visited for many years. However, this woman was obviously aware that Grace had owned more artifacts than those which were still in the house.

"The lawyer should have told you, at the reading of the will. Grace, Mrs Sanderson, very kindly left her pictures and one or two pieces of furniture to me when she died. I was not expecting anything like that, so when the lawyer telephoned…"

"You mean to say that you were given all the oil paintings and watercolours which came from my stepmother's estate, after knowing her for a total of, what is it, three, four years."

"Four. Six months of which she spent in bed and I came in daily to check on her progress."

"Well this is ridiculous – and I see that most of my father's paintings have gone. What did you persuade her to do with them? Burn them or sell them."

"I'm sorry, I don't like your tone of voice, Miss Sanderson. If you need to know anything else, please ask your lawyer when you see him. I'm afraid I am unable to help you further" and Jane stood up, gesturing toward the door. The little woman stood up and bustled through the doorway.

"We'll see about that!" she said, over her shoulder, as Jane held open the front door and she rattled off down the stony drive. When she was alone, Jane sat down once more and twiddled the ties of her discarded apron, while she considered this visit. Surely the family had been at the reading of the will and surely Miss Sanderson knew exactly what had happened to the contents of the house. It was bad enough that Grace had arranged for her granny's house to transfer into her husband's name and therefore the redoubtable Miss Sanderson would inherit any proceeds of the sale. She must be a very greedy woman to want Grace's personal belongings as well – and to more or less accuse her of some kind of illegal persuasion. Her reason for the call must have been a warning, that she was going to seek legal advice regarding the items left to Jane. She must have forgotten that Grace had left her some money also.

Never having discussed Grace with Michael, she had several sleepless nights thinking of the situation which had arisen out of her friendship with a lonely old neighbour. Admittedly, he would have been the ideal person to frighten the step-daughter away forever, with his cold, logical mind but she could hardly involve him at this late stage. He was vague enough about her inheritance and merely waved his hand in the air, saying,

"Find somewhere to put those dabbles where I won't be annoyed by their presence. Either that, or sell them and I'll bank the money for you."

Her money from Grace had been banked, quite easily he would be surprised to hear, all by herself, in an account in her own name. When Rob appeared in the garden next door, she called him over and told him she must talk with him, in the summerhouse. He had never seen her refurbished hideaway and was amazed when she led him into the small, comfortable space and closed the glass doors behind them. It was the ideal place to be together, away from everything and everybody.

CHAPTER 26

Jane's life with Michael had settled into an easy-going routine. Her boys seemed happy at George Heriot's school and tackled their studies diligently and Jane lived for the times when she and Rob entered the sanctum of the summerhouse together, which had become two or three times a week. They talked extensively about garden design, planting techniques and the animals and wildlife to be seen in and around the two large gardens.

She had continued to write her journal in a commonplace book, which she kept in the sea chest. The thought that Rob sat on top of her recent life brought a smile to her lips because it summed up her feelings for him; he dominated her everyday existence.

One afternoon in the early summer, just before school broke up for its long summer holiday, Andrew barged into the kitchen, schoolbag hanging from his shoulder, cap askew and his tie knot over the point of the collar of his once pale blue shirt.

"Mother?" he started, long before he was completely inside the room and still closing the back-door. "Mother, I have decided to join the Boys' Brigade."

Thinking this was a good idea, she gave him her full attention and beckoned him to sit down at the table opposite her, where she had been doing some mending.

"I know you'll think I should join the cadet corps at school but I am determined to join the BBs, so I can go to meetings here, or rather nearby, in the village."

"Isn't that rather silly, darling? Shouldn't you join something at school, so you can be with your new friends?"

"That's just the point. I don't have many new friends and I would much rather meet boys from Uphall I knew when I was wee."

"This sounds like a step backwards, Andrew. I can't imagine your father allowing this."

"Do we have to tell him, Mother?"

"Oh, my dear boy. Don't ask me to lie for you."

"Then don't lie, just don't mention it. Please. Please. It will only be one meeting a week – and maybe some outings when school packs up. And I must have something to do during the long break."

Jane was torn. If Michael found out she was encouraging Andrew to hang around the village again, there would be hell to pay but if she refused to condone Andrew's individualism, he would probably go off and do something stupid and most probably lie to her as well. As it was, she was still his confidante.

"Alright, Andrew, but there it must end. I don't want to hear about any forays down to the burn or outings into the countryside with boys from the village. You know I have nothing against them but your father is adamant that you will make friends of your own station."

"Huh! My own station. All I want to do is be accepted by the chaps I meet, who live near me. I don't want a different station in life from them. I want to be one of the lads."

"Enough said. You have my permission to join the Boys' Brigade and nothing more."

Jane wondered how the local boys would treat someone who went to a private school in Edinburgh. Chances were that they would find him a total snob and he would give up the BBs as soon as he joined.

That did not happen, however. He went along to join up that weekend and came home singing a marching song, telling his brother how stupid he was for not joining with him but Henry merely shrugged his shoulders. There was a uniform of a cap and sash, which had to be worn over something dark-coloured at parades and Jane was glad to notice that Andrew had become proud of looking smart at last.

Michael never asked what the boys were doing in their spare time, so the subject remained a secret between the three of them. Henry had proved himself capable of keeping confidences and, in fact, appeared to be uninterested in anything but his own life.

Jane was still subjected to argumentative behaviour from Michael but it became very one-sided. Whenever he attempted to correct her or to ridicule her, she remained silent and let him shout and hold his private tantrums whenever he felt moved to do so. Luckily, he only started his tumultuous commotions when the boys were in bed and hopefully asleep, so there was only Jane left to handle them. She sometimes wondered whether he was altogether sane but he could hardly hold down an important job and handle his staff if he had gone mad.

000

It was a warm, balmy summer evening and Michael had gone into Edinburgh, Henry was staying with a school friend for a couple of nights and Andrew had gone to Dunbar with the Boys' Brigade. After he had been a member for several months and had displayed exemplary behaviour, Jane had decided to come clean and tell Michael what he was doing, couching her explanation in words he wanted to hear, such as discipline, rigorous training and officer material. There had been no outburst at all, which amazed her.

The sun was lowering in an orange and blue sky, turning the few clouds a gentle pink on their undersides and bathing the garden in soft shadows. Birds were flitting here and there, from nest to tree and back again and there was a warm feel to everything. Having finished her work for the day, she decided to wander down to the summerhouse and write her journal in the fading rays of the sun. That corner of the garden tended to hold the light for longer than any other part and she knew that there would be enough left for her to write a page or so.

She opened the door and lifted the long cushion from the sea chest. Her hiding place was secure, as long as no-one took the time to investigate the small, interior drawers and she doubted whether anyone in the family would think of walking right to the end of their plot, let alone move a firmly attached cushion from an obvious garden-room seat. She extricated her current journal and flicked to the last page. Moving back to the first entry in the diary, she noted that it had started when Grace was still living next door and refused to read it in case she was thrust from her relaxed, happiness into sadness once more.

Her pen was poised to fill in the date, when a shadow covered the sun and she looked up to check whether a cloud was about to move away. There was no cloud, just the tall figure of Rob, in silhouette, in front of the glass doors. Her heart started to pound and her face flushed, primarily at being caught out with her secret but also because she had thought him miles away. To see him here, in her garden, without warning, gave her a feeling of déjà vu, not because it had ever happened before in reality but because this is what happened in her dreams, as she lay on her own, lonely side of the bed every night.

"Hello, Mrs Donaldson," he drawled and brushed back his hair with those wonderful strong, brown hands.

"Don't call me that!" she said, more irritably than she had meant to.

"Sorry. I caught you at a bad time. I'll be on my way."

"No! Don't go, Rob. You know why I was annoyed – that name! Come in and sit down. What brings you here at this time anyway?"

She noticed that he had changed into smarter clothes than he usually wore when working. He wore a bright white shirt with a collar this time and moleskin trousers in a pale shade of brown and his feet were clad in shoes, not boots.

"I happened to see your husband driving off on the main road into Edinburgh so I did my arithmetic and decided he would be gone for some time – and knowing the boys were otherwise engaged, thought you might like some company. Finding you in our summerhouse was just a bonus; I expected to have to persuade you to go for a walk with me."

"I'm so glad you came, Rob. It's the first time we've been together in the evening and even now it's not quite dark." She noted that he had called it 'our' summerhouse.

"No and you seem to be busy. If I'm interrupting anything, just give me my marching orders."

"I would hardly do that," she said, head down then looking up, knowing she was being flirtatious for the first time in years. It must be the evening light and the presence of the man she loved appearing as if in one of her dreams. There, she had admitted it to herself, she was in love with Rob.

He came inside and sat down on the sea chest, long legs splayed out. He leaned back onto the wall and ran his hand through his hair, which had blonded naturally in the sun. Jane tried to finish writing a sentence but realised that it was out of the question, so she pushed her book under the cushion of her cane seat and leaned forward slightly. Rob said nothing, merely lounged and stared. This was dreadful. They were sitting opposite each other as the sun went down and there was not a single person anywhere around. All their conversation topics, which were discussed at length during the day, seemed too facile and he did not appear to want to talk anyway. She repositioned herself, leaning back to mirror his image and their eyes rested on each other. Jane was the first to break.

"You seem very melancholy," she said.
"No."
"Then what?"
"Apprehensive."
"Why?"
"I'm wondering how you will react when I pull you across here and kiss you."
"Oh" she said. "It can never happen again, Rob." But she was hoping it would.

He stood up and covered his face with both his hands, rubbing his eyes and letting his fingers move down his cheeks, until they fell from his chin.

"I'm sorry! I'm sorry!" he said, suddenly and reverted to a kneeling position, his hands once more covering his handsome face. Through his fingers, he mumbled something about her married state and how he hadn't intended this to happen and all Jane felt was a colossal sense of frustration, an agony of loss, which left her bereft and tearful. "My dear, darling Jane. I am so sorry to have done this to you, when you have been so loving, so wonderful…"

She had known how to handle disappointment from an early age. She had been promised treats, outings, even her marriage, and had had to come to terms with loss; this was just another rejection. Sitting up and smoothing her skirt, feeling around for her shoes which had somehow fallen off, and running her fingers through her hair, she composed her face and smiled cheerfully.

"It's alright Rob. It was my fault. I should never have led you on. Now – why don't we go into the house and have a glass of my home-made lemonade or perhaps something a little stronger," she said, trying to be the hostess and attempting to banish the ridiculous little scene from her mind.

"No – no. I'll be on my way and leave you in peace," he said solemnly. Then, with a quick glance and an apologetic smile, he opened the door and left.

Jane stood there, upset, tearful, worried. And then she remembered her New Year's Resolution. But she had not figured on the combination of a beautiful night sky, the absence of her family and the proximity of Rob. Yet she had kept her resolution; why had she because she knew she loved him.

CHAPTER 27

The bedroom door creaked. It always had. If Michael had taken the trouble to oil it, she would be unaware of the late nights he was keeping because, once her head hit the pillow, Jane was right out for the count. When she heard the creak though, she knew that he had returned in the early hours of the morning; not only that but she could smell perfume on his hair and it was totally different from her own Chanel No.5, given to her many years ago – her precious bottle kept for special occasions, which never materialized. He went out three or four times a week now and she wondered why he continued to behave as if everything were normal.

He held a sensible conversation during breakfast and cautioned the boys about their conduct at school – just as he always had – then he took the car out of the garage and drove off down the road. When the house was empty, she cleared breakfast and wondered what to do. The garden was the obvious choice but a garden without Rob seemed empty. Since their foolish interlude in the summerhouse, he had been nowhere near and her mind had raced on to imagine him with someone else, someone free, who had no irksome husband and sons to consider. A single man was entitled to something better than a married woman with children in tow. At first she had expected him to appear during working time, so they could have discussed their problem in the cold light of day but it had been some weeks now and there was no sign of him. No gardening had been done next door, now Grace had gone.

Just as she had ejected him from her thoughts when he had gone off to Edinburgh to work, she would do so again. He was a dream, a fantasy, an hallucination and she must put a stop to this speculation before she ruined what was left of her tarnished marriage. All she wanted now was to live in peace, in her beautiful house with its precious garden, with her two wonderful sons; the fact that Michael had to be included in the package was immaterial. As soon as the boys were old enough to cope without her, they could arrange something amicable.

And perhaps by then Michael would have decided to leave her for one of his women. But surely, he would never leave this house and she would be the one on the compost heap.

000

So time moved on, in its ruthless way, until Andrew was the first one to leave school and he took a job which his father had arranged for him at the offices of Scottish Oil; Henry remained in the sixth form. It was not ideal but Andrew accepted it anyway, not seeming to have much ambition for anything – apart, that is, from his interest in the Boys' Brigade. His employment was local and therefore meant he could continue to live at home and attend BB meetings regularly.

Over the years, Mrs Sanderson's stepdaughter had enlisted the services of a lawyer in Edinburgh, who happened to be a young, attractive person, so Jane enjoyed his visits rather than dreading them. The first time she had heard the doorbell and seen the shadow of a tall figure through the stained glass inner door, she had run to answer it, expecting it to be Rob, so she was caught at sixes and sevens by the smart young man.

"I...I'm sorry. I thought you were somebody else," she said and was surprised to find him holding back a smile, as he stood on the doorstep in his dark suit, holding a black briefcase.

"I almost wish I had been," he replied and then put the shutters over any glimmer of amusement, before saying,

"I have come at the behest of Miss Sanderson to enquire about the whereabouts of certain items belonging to her stepmother, Mrs Grace Sanderson. It is imperative that you understand that all artifacts belonging to the said Mrs Sanderson are returned to their rightful owner, by which I mean Miss Sanderson. All the property of Mrs Grace Sanderson was left to her stepdaughter at the time of her death and any instructions by word of mouth must be ignored in favour of the Last Will and Testament, which was placed in the hands of McLean, Macdonald and Farquharson at the time."

Jane expected him to take a deep breath after reciting all this mumbo-jumbo but he was quite unaffected and waited patiently for her to answer.

"I expect you should come in Mr...Mr... I'm sorry I don't have your name."

"Farquharson. I am the junior partner of the firm of lawyers in Edinburgh. Pleased to make your acquaintance." He held out his hand and Jane, feeling utterly ridiculous, took it, noting that it felt large, warm and dry – not at all the insipid hand of an office worker.

They went into the sitting room and he sat exactly where the bustling Miss Sanderson had carefully placed herself some time ago. Putting down his briefcase at the side of his chair, he placed both hands on the arms and looked directly at Jane. This time he allowed his expression to soften, as he said,

"I'm sorry about this, Mrs Donaldson. I'm sure it was an understandable mistake and it can easily be rectified. If you would just give me the paintings and let me see the pieces of furniture, I can report back to my partners and the whole sordid business will be terminated."

"I'm sorry as well, Mr Farquharson. The pictures left to me by Grace were given in an act of friendship and for a definite reason. I was under the impression that the gift had been put in writing; it was certainly in her will. She wanted them to be cared for by someone who would value them and not sold for profit by her money-grabbing step daughter." She was amazed at the way her thoughts came out, without any dissembling or hypocrisy. "As for the pieces of furniture, they held sentimental value for my friend because the two items – a sewing box and a small Pembroke table - belonged to her mother and grandmother before her and also had sentimental value."

"In that case, you leave me no alternative but to fight this case in a court of law."

"Fight away but you will find that what I have said is the truth. Also, I will stand up in court and explain exactly how few times your client, Miss Sanderson, visited her stepmother and how she left her to fend for herself every Christmas and after two accidents when she was hospitalised." Jane could feel herself becoming more and more furious and it was only due to the fact that the lawyer was a pleasant man of about her own age that she held back further comments.

"I had no idea... From what she said, Grace Sanderson and her step daughter were the best of friends and everything in the house was left to her, more or less as a thank you for her care at the end."

"Oh no. That is a pack of lies. The woman is mercenary and could hardly wait until she got her hands on her dead father's possessions, as soon as Grace died. The house actually belonged to Grace's family but she put it in his name when they married because she was such a generous person. I'm sorry, I shouldn't be talking like this to you, her lawyer, but I can't help myself."

"That's alright, Mrs Donaldson but I feel I must take a few notes of all you have said, so I can report back in detail. Would you mind if we go through it again, so I am clear of the facts?"

Jane said she did not mind and even went to get them a tray of tea, while he made his notes. Then, feeling he should be totally in the picture, she took him into the living room across the hall and showed him the pile of ten pictures, all interspersed with newspaper against breakage, awaiting a time when she could hang them, and the two small items of furniture.

"That's all I have left of my friend," she said, sadly.

He touched her on the shoulder, lightly and said,

"I'll see what can be done," before collecting his case and bidding her farewell.

She stood in the doorway, smiling after him and she knew that he would sort out this dreadful mess. He was that kind of person. What a fine figure of a man he was – tall and spare, with a pale complexion no doubt from too much office work, short dark hair which was straight and plastered down with grease but unlikely soft grey eyes, which were prone to a twinkle. Mr Farquharson was the best lawyer Miss Sanderson could have employed and she hoped he would tell her a few home truths, albeit couched in his out-of-date legal jargon.

000

That night, Andrew came home from work with his father and announced he was going on a weekend camping outing near Dunbar. Michael listened vaguely and hardly said a word, so Jane figured that his mind was on other things.

Jane was pleased for two reasons: Andrew would enjoy his freedom and take benefit from a couple of days in the fresh sea air and she could spend some time with Henry, who had become dreadfully introspective recently and totally academic. He was starting Edinburgh University after the holidays and she wanted to be sure that he was not worrying about such a big change in his circumstances. He had decided to study medical science – not because he favoured a career as a doctor but more as a researcher. His schoolwork had been praiseworthy and Jane felt that he would succeed famously. Studying was his forte and he was prone to shutting himself up for hours on end to ensure that he passed examinations with flying colours. If he was a few marks away from top of his class in any subject, he tended to agonise for days, sometimes weeks and she was intent on helping him to relax out of this fastidious frame of mind. This weekend would help.

The next few evenings were spent ironing clothes she had washed during the day, standing at the poss-tub for hours, over summer shirts and many pairs of socks found at the backs of drawers and amid the dust under Andrew's bed. He was determined to be the smartest corporal in his unit and flattered Jane regarding the whiteness of her wash, until she felt she had to live up to his expectations. As she pushed items through the mangle and hung them up to dry in the bright sunshine, she wondered why she did not ask Mrs Morgan to do such exhausting tasks but it was a rhetorical question.

The day eventually arrived when Andrew donned his Boys' Brigade uniform, took his bags, one in each hand, and walked off down the drive to the main road, where the bus was to collect him. As she watched him, straight-backed and handsome, in the guise of a soldier, Jane's heart skipped a beat. He was her child, her son, flesh of her flesh. Did she want him to grow up so soon? It hardly felt like eighteen years since she had borne him and yet, in some ways, it seemed as if she had been married and had children for many more than that.

Henry had not come down to say goodbye to his brother, preferring to remain in his room reading but she was sure they had exchanged a few words before Andrew went. They were not what you would call close brothers but they held the same feelings of loyalty towards each other and each one knew he had a friend on which to call, should the need arise.

As Jane closed the stained-glass door downstairs, Henry went back to his books, having watched his tall brother from his window, until he was out of sight. He was the only one who knew the main reason for Andrew's fierce determination to climb the ladder of rank in the Boys' Brigade. He just wanted to be the best in everything he did. In that way they were very similar, the only difference being that Andrew gave up if he knew he would never be the best, whereas Henry put everything into his endeavours, knowing he could be.

CHAPTER 28

The Boys Brigade camp was erected by the boys in a farmer's field at West Barnes, just above the sand-dunes which proclaimed the shoreline. As they were lifting tent poles and pushing in stakes to prevent the easterly wind from thoroughly chilling them at night, the Advance Party boys took surreptitious glances at the wide expanse of sand and the long peninsular, or was it an island, beyond the grey-green water. It was easy to imagine the line of trees to be palms and the piece of land out there a desert island but unfortunately, even in summer, the weather was too cool to be anywhere exotic. It was not exactly cold and even quite mild for the coast of Scotland but, even so, not a tropical climate.

"Come on Squad, put your backs into it!" yelled Andrew, enjoying playing the part of Corporal. He had been made up in rank recently, due to the way he seemed to be able to organise the other boys better than most and he was enjoying putting it into practice. Tomorrow morning he would 'tell off' the boys into parts of a platoon and decide who would be Section Commanders. This was a lot better than working in an office.

When the canvas village was completed, they had time to walk around their boundaries and the officers gathered together to plan where to build fires, where to position latrines and how to arrange the following day. The Captain sat them down in a circle and lectured them about good behaviour and what not to accept from the lower ranks, then left them alone to discuss strategies but not until he had stood up and said the Boys Brigade motto about four times. When he left, the young officers turned to each other and said, 'Sure and Steadfast' in different tones of voice and different accents, until they all dissolved into crazy laughter. Then, looking around to make sure that they had not been overheard, they settled down to make some decisions about the following morning. The main party was due to arrive in a bus on Monday, when hopefully all tents had been erected and the camp had begun to look more organised. So, after deciding that ball games would be played by the advance party the following morning at low tide, Andrew and two others went for a walk around the perimeter fencing.

"Look over there, lads! There's an encampment of Girl Guides in the next field!" Alex said, in some excitement.

"So there is!" said his friend, leaning on the fence and peering into the distance.

"I wonder how many there are? What age do they start Guides, Alex?" Andrew asked.

"Eleven or twelve I think but they go on 'til about sixteen or more – and there's always the officers. They might be tasty."

"It doesn't matter whether they are or not. We won't get a minute to ourselves with this rabble – and the old white rat will keep his eye open for anything untoward, I'll bet."

"Hark at him. What's this 'untoward' business, Andy? Is that what they taught you at that posh school in the 'burgh and kindly show a bit of respect for Captain White, if you please, my boy!"

"I just meant he won't let us get our leg over... the fence, you know what I mean."

"Aye, I ken what'ch mean, man. Now come back to earth and talk normal, will you?"

"Aye. It's due to being around my old man so much. I wish I'd never taken on that job at his place – it's turning me into a pansy."

"I hope not," said Dougie, with a grin. "Let's have a bet on who gets to them girls the first."

"You're on!" the two others said in unison and they slapped hands to cinch the deal.

As they scuffed through the long grass back to the tents, the rest of the Company was running along the fence line, having been to look at the sea – a sight some of them only saw at camp. Their voices were full of animation and Andrew had not the heart to stop them from enthusing. He had only been to the seaside a few times himself before he joined up and then had not been allowed to paddle, in case he covered himself in sand and sea water. No doubt his mother would have let them take off their shoes and socks to go in but his stern father had been there on each occasion.

Fires were lit and the food cooked in a bit of a practice run; bangers and beans was to be their standard diet for much of the week, with the addition of eggs, eggs, eggs and a bit of bacon. After everyone went to their tents, which was early due to the busy day, the three conspirators sat in the dark and planned their foray into the adjoining field.

"Our first trip has to be a recce, just to see what's on offer. If they're all scrawny school kids, we won't bother, eh men?" Alex said in a whisper.

"Naw. I don't fancy picking up jail bait," reiterated Dougie.

"Well, we'll soon find out after the sussing-out campaign," said Andrew.

"Sshh! This has to be deadly secret. Not a word has to get out to the ranks or to the Captain. Agreed?"

"Aye, of course," they all nodded and wrapped themselves in their sleeping bags for the night.

000

During that week, back at home, Jane and Henry got on extremely well. He appeared to be relaxing into his role of only child and spent much more time downstairs than he usually did. He still had his head permanently hidden in a book but Jane noticed with delight that he had started reading a Sherlock Holmes novel and the school books were kept upstairs.

"I'm glad to have some time with you this holiday, Henry. When you start University, I don't suppose you'll have time for anything or anybody."

"I'll still have time for you Mother," he said unexpectedly and Jane came forward and gave him a hug. "The reason for all my studying is that I desperately want to do well for myself and the only way I can handle it is to go off by myself and cram the stuff in."

"I know my darling but you have to save some time for yourself as well. I would love to see you playing football or cricket sometimes and not just hiding away with your books."

"Time enough when I get my degree."

"I have every confidence in you and know in my heart of hearts that you will succeed... Oh! Do I hear your father coming. I must get the meal ready."

"Why do you always run around after him, Mother? Surely there's plenty of time before dinner."

"Never mind, my dear. I have my own reasons for making things smooth."

"I'll bet you do," he muttered, as he collected his book and sloped away, thinking she wouldn't want to suffer a beating when they were in bed together.

000

The next morning, Mr Farquharson rang the doorbell and, this time Jane had no thoughts in her head as to who it would be. She had decided to behave in a more seemly manner, if not for Henry, for herself. Mooning around like a schoolgirl would do no good at all.

"Good morning, Mrs Donaldson. I promised to keep you informed about the progress of your contretemps with Miss Sanderson and here I am."

She hadn't expected him to drive all the way out to Uphall to tell her the news.

"How good of you, Mr Farquharson. Do come in."

"Thank you," he said, removing his charcoal grey, brimmed hat. She took it from him and hung it on the hallstand, feeling the ghost of a housemaid inhabit her for a minute. They walked through to the sunny sitting room and she motioned him to sit down.

"I would ring for morning coffee, if I had a maid," she smiled "but if you are content to wait, I'll get it myself. I feel ready for a break." He nodded.

Walking off through what used to be the baize door, she grinned to herself. Here I am entertaining a man again but this time I haven't the tiniest feeling of guilt, whereas if it were Rob... oh, oh, this was dangerous ground. She made a pot of coffee, putting cups and saucers on a tray, then entered her sitting room once more.

"I was just admiring your delightful garden, sorry." he said, turning away from the bay window. He was the kind of man who said sorry in every sentence, as if he were constantly treading on peoples' toes.

"It's quite alright, Mr Farquharson. I love my garden and spend a great deal of time either in it or just looking out at it, deciding what I will do next."

"If only I had a garden…" he muttered.

"I suppose you live in town, do you?"

"Yes, I'm sorry to say, right in the centre, in a fourth-floor flat."

That answered the next question. He was a single man. No woman in his wife's position would live in a fourth-floor apartment.

"Poor you," she said and poured them some steaming coffee.

"The reason I came out here personally is because I feel bad about the way I handled your problem the last time we met. I hardly gave you a chance to explain matters, sorry. When I reported back to my partners and the papers were perused once more, we came to the conclusion that Miss Sanderson was acting out of some personal vendetta, rather than making a valid legal claim. You will be pleased to know that you will hear no more about it. She has been informed of the implications. I'm so sorry to have confused you."

He finished his speech with a clearing of the throat and Jane wondered why he had not become a barrister, rather than one of the back-room boys.

"Thank you very much Mr Farquharson. It was so kind of you to take so much interest in what must be a very small part of your busy workload. Thank you again."

"Now that all the legal business is at an end, do you think we could dispense with the Mr Farquharson bit? It is rather a mouthful. My name's Kenneth – call me Ken."

How weird. The familiarity had come along too late. What was the point of exchanging first names if they were never going to use them.

"Please, call me Jane but I feel we will hardly meet again, er, Ken. Didn't you say you lived in Edinburgh and Ecclesmachan is not exactly the kind of place you would visit, unless you had to."

"But Uphall is. You see, I omitted to mention that my old mother lives down the road and I come over here to see her regularly."

"How nice. You must come in for a cup of tea when you're passing," she said in her best country lady's voice, hoping he would and yet dreading his arriving when Michael was at home.

They finished their coffee and Ken went off to his motorcar. Henry watched him moving down the drive and wondered what was happening. His mother had no sooner stopped having long conversations with next-door's gardener, when she had started entertaining this tall, formal-looking man. Perhaps his father had reason to shout and yell every so often.

CHAPTER 29

Rob had immersed himself in work. There was a definite need for gardeners in the area, by owners of all the large mansion houses hidden away in woods and copses, so he hardly found it necessary to drive down the Ecclesmachan road. Work was the one thing which took away his personal contemplations, allowing him to concentrate on the matter in hand – whether it be planting a new tree or pruning an old one. Unfortunately, when it came to splitting large conglomerations of plants or wheeling his barrow to the compost heap, jobs he did regularly, the picture of Jane came to him. Why had he run off from their summerhouse? There was a deep-rooted conviction inside him which forbade him to take on a serious relationship and even he was unsure why.

Although it was the wrong time of year for it, he felt the need for some hard, heavy digging, so he investigated his orders for the day and came to the conclusion that his client's old asparagus bed would benefit from some strenuous work.

Double-digging was a job he normally left until the end of the season, when he could turn over the clods of earth and let the hard night frosts break down the soil into a more friable consistency. But breaking it up with a fork would help him to put his thoughts in order, so he collected together his spade, fork and weed bucket and got started. Each time he placed his boot on top of the steel blade and pushed it into the ground, he had that wonderful feeling of freedom, a sensation of demolishing the old, in preparation for creating the new. Of all the occupations in the world, gardening was the one which gave a man the chance to explore innovation and bury the spent parts of life deep in the ground beneath his feet.

It was about half way down the rectangular bed that the revolutionary thought presented itself. The reason why he could not give himself totally to any woman had been hidden in the darkest, undisclosed recesses of his brain; it was no wonder that he had been unable to reach it. By refusing to think and by working his body to its limit, the explanation for his feeble escapism had come to him. Now, he could work out an answer.

000

"Why not meet me for a midnight dip?" Andrew said to the attractive young Girl Guide. "I'm sure you're a courageous girl who could work out a way to escape from your tent-mates. How about it? After all, that's what going off to camp is all about – using your initiative. Our Captain keeps telling us that over and over."

"I don't know. What if we're caught, Andrew?"

"Surely you don't think I would arrange anything unless I was absolutely sure. The officers all go off to their tents to talk about us after supper. They can't fool me. What about tonight, after lights-out? Go on Stephanie."

He was determined to win the bet and had befriended this nice-looking girl, Stephanie, almost as soon as the three pals had gone their separate ways, when they were in Dunbar buying provisions. She had been in the greengrocers when he walked past on the way to the dairy and he had done a double-take, then turned in his tracks. Her hair had been hitched up at the back in a couple of hair-slides, which he was sure were not normal Girl Guide uniform, so he thought she would be fair game; anyone who could flout a little rule might be convinced to do the same with a bigger one. He would persuade her to meet him in the sand dunes this evening. That would be half-way there.

"Oh alright Andy," she said, after some more sweet talk from him. "But just make sure we get back without being seen. My mother would go mad if I was sent home for behaving badly." Mum usually could not care less where she went and who she met; she was quoting her own morals, not her mother's. But Andrew seemed to be a nice boy and a bit of excitement never did anyone any harm, within reason of course.

"Right you are. I'll meet you here tonight at eleven o'clock. It should be really dark then and there's no moon tonight because I checked."

"You were very certain of yourself, weren't you?"

"I always am – you'll see."

"Now, no monkey business or I'm not coming," she said, flirtatiously, hoping she was putting her point across, without sounding like a spoil-sport.

"Do I look like a monkey. Just a little swim in that lovely cool water, when both camps are fast asleep – that's all I'm looking for – a bit of adventure."

Then Stephanie slipped back over the fence.

The hours until lights-out were long and boring. Andrew drifted through them without really understanding what he was doing, neither in the game of rounders nor the camp quiz which followed tea but eventually he made a big deal about stretching and yawning in his sleeping bag and burying his head in his home-made pillow. The other two had no idea he was going out tonight and he had heard them making preliminary plans for tomorrow, to cross the field where the Guides were, so they could meet a couple of girls. Wait until they found out.

He must have checked his watch with his torch under the covers about ten times before the long hand reached a quarter-to. He was determined not to sit around waiting for too long, so Stephanie would not mark him down as desperate. It was important that she wanted to meet him more than he wanted her. He might be young but he had studied the ways of the world and most older boys of his acquaintance seemed to keep their girls if they treated them with a casual air. The more they had to struggle, the more they tended to hang on.

The path down through the dunes was well-trodden by the many feet of boys and girls during the day, so it was easy to figure out the way to the tallest, sandy hill. He fought against the desire to whistle as he strode along and noted that the sky had become nicely overcast and there was not a star to be seen. Had he not known the route, he would have found it impossible to negotiate the last few yards onto the soft sand.

"Psst! Hello! I'm here," he heard a voice whisper in the pitch dark. Good, she wanted to see him.

"Oh hello Stephanie. You made it then?"

"Yes. It was very easy."

"I told you it would be. Everybody else is totally exhausted. They'll sleep like the dead until morning."

"I feel a bit tired myself," she said feebly, wishing she had curled up in her sleeping bag instead of flouting all the rules of camping that were ever made.

"What you need is a swim in the briny, to wake you up. Let's get our gear off and go in straight away."

"What do you mean? How much gear off? I brought my swimming costume."

"Cozies are for cissies. I'm going in in the buff. Come on, be brave."

"But...but you're a boy!"

"Yes and you're a girl. We are a bit different but who cares."

This was not what Stephanie had anticipated and whatever Andrew said, she would never take off her clothes in front of anybody, let alone a boy she had just met.

"Here, have a slug of this. It'll warm you up and you won't even think of your bathing suit." He offered her the half-bottle of whisky he had bought in Dunbar. It was not something he ever did but a little sip of alcohol was supposed to remove inhibitions, he had heard.

It was certainly very cold and her mum often had a little drink of gin if she felt chilly. So, she took the bottle and put it up to her mouth tentatively. Then she poured it in and spluttered all over the sand. The little spits of whisky sank into the soft, pale sand, making a random design of dots in front of them. It was dreadful stuff. It tasted the way you imagined tobacco did if you smoked.

"Hey, don't waste it. That cost good money, you know," Andrew blustered, starting to feel rather foolish now that the adventure was underway. What would his mother think of him now?

"Sorry, Andy. It's just that it tasted so strong. I've only ever had sherry before."

"It'll be alright on the next sip. Here, have another go."

This time she tasted it and tipped it back a bit further, then a bit more and a bit more. She was getting the hang of this and he had not even tried it.

"My turn I think, before you drink it all."

He put the bottle to his lips, thinking this had just been on her mouth. Then, as if he drank whisky all the time, he lifted up the bottle and had a huge swig. It certainly was strong but he must not cough and splutter if he wanted her to think he was a man of the world.

"Right! Let's be on our way."

They took off their clothes, Stephanie hiding behind her towel to put on her swimming costume. Andrew chickened-out at the last minute and pranced around foolishly in his Y-fronts.

The whisky had started to do its job, making Stephanie feel warmer and less inhibited, so she ran fast into the waves. Andrew ran after her and they entered the calmer sea beyond the soft waves together, holding hands and laughing into each other's faces.

After a short time in the freezing cold water, Andrew grabbed her hand and pulled her back to the shore, saying,

"What about another warming drop of whisky before we get dressed?"

Stephanie didn't need any coaxing, due to the extreme cold, so when they were back in the dunes, sitting on the towel Andrew had brought and, drinking the warming liquid, he put his arms around her bare shoulders. This was the first time he had felt a girl's flesh, although he had pretended to be a man of the world. The hilarity and banter they had indulged in previously just disintegrated, as Andrew pulled himself away from a now tearful girl.

"What's the matter, Stephanie? I'm not going to hurt you." He was starting to feel sorry for what he had instigated and realised that the girl in front of him, dressed only in her bathing suit, was a really nice girl. She was honest and moral and had trusted him implicitly. That was before he had encouraged her to drink strong liquor. He should be ashamed of himself. He *was* ashamed of himself and he had no idea how to comfort her, without seeming to be pushy. He grabbed at his clothing and flung it on feverishly, then found her pile of discarded blue serge and handed it to her in a lump.

"You'd better get dressed, so I can get you back to your camp," he said seriously. "We've done what we planned to do and it's all over now."

"I don't feel well," she said.

"Well, you're in the right place and you have no clothes to mess up, so get on with it."

"I don't mean really sick. I'm just worried that they know I'm missing. I daren't go back."

"Don't be soft. It was only a bit of fun and no-one will know. Now put your gear on and get back to your tent before anybody knows you're missing." He felt like an old hand at this subterfuge lark, although he had never done anything like it before. But she didn't know that. She must think he was truly sophisticated and even experienced.

They walked up the path from the sand-dunes silently and when they came to the perimeter fence of the BB's camp, Andrew took her hand and skirted round it to the gate leading into the Guides' field. She was shaking and he could not decide whether it was from fear or cold.

"Go on Stephanie. Get yourself back to camp. You'll soon warm up – and thanks for coming for a swim – it was good fun. No doubt I'll see you around before we go back."

She looked round disconsolately, rubbing her eyes with her sandy cardigan sleeve and waved at him coyly, before turning to run quietly along the boundary fence towards her tent. That was it then. He'd won the bet.

CHAPTER 30

Andrew returned home from camp thoroughly exhausted, both physically, due to the games they all played constantly, and mentally, mostly because after winning the bet he had not been able to get Stephanie out of his mind. The other boys had decided to give it a miss when he reported back the following morning that he alone had succeeded, so they threw themselves into the exertions of camp life and forgot about the Girl Guides completely – except Andrew, who discovered he had fallen hook, line and sinker for a girl in her bathing costume in the cold waves of the North Sea.

Jane was surprised that she now had two serious-minded sons, not knowing that the change in her younger boy had evolved in the process of growing-up, being in charge of other boys and meeting a girl. He gave a long, detailed description of the Boys' Brigade camp, mentioning several of his fellow-officers by name, then it was as if it had never happened. He also took to his room more frequently, so for Jane it was like living in an empty house.

When the back door knocker rattled, she was in the kitchen, baking, and she rubbed her floury hands on her apron, thinking it was the coalman. She was stunned into silence when she found Rob on the wide, cement step, with a sack flung casually over his shoulder.

"I thought you might like some bulbs for the front garden," he said, then broke into his contagious wide smile. "Not really – I just thought it would be a good excuse if your husband turned up, or the boys saw me."

"Both boys are upstairs and Michael's away for the day in Glasgow. Come in for a cool drink, Rob."

"Could we take it down to the summerhouse? I have something to say to you."

"Alright – lemonade alright for you?"

"Fine. I'll go down there."

She could hardly hold the bottle, as she poured two glasses of her own home-made lemonade. She put them on a small tin tray but found they rattled around too much in her nervousness, so took one in each hand and pushed the door closed with her behind. There was no point in telling Andrew and Henry where she was because they would not care; they often left the house themselves and disappeared for hours on end without saying a word. This was her chance to get her own back on the two of them.

When she arrived at her little hideaway, Rob had seen her coming and held the door open. He took both glasses and parked them on an upturned box and positioned himself opposite on the sea chest.

"This is quite a surprise," Jane said, more coldly than she felt.

"I know. I wouldn't blame you if you told me to go away. Jane, I had to see you. You know how I was the last time we were here..."

"I could hardly forget. You made me feel very upset..."

"Don't Jane, please. I didn't understand myself then. It took me all this time to realise why I acted that way – but now I think I know and I want to tell you. I wanted so much to be with you. Can you understand?"

He was so upset, so confused, not like himself at all, that Jane felt sorry for him and said,

"Please don't worry, Rob. I am interested in what you have to say and I'm sorry for being so hard-faced just now."

"It wasn't easy coming here, my dear."

She liked that, 'my dear'.

"It wasn't easy at all, in fact I think it's the most difficult thing I've ever done. I just had to tell you... I love you, Jane."

His handsome face was creased-up in desperation and he looked down at his boots, as if he were ashamed of saying something so marvellous.

"I love you too," she said, softly "and I thought I'd lost you."

"You can't get rid of me so easily," he quipped, reverting back to his usual jokey self.

"I hope not," she said, absolutely seriously but with a smile. This was the best day of her life and it looked as though Rob felt the same.

He reached over and pulled her towards him, exactly as he had the last, unforgettable time. She sat beside him on the sea chest and rested her head on his shoulder, enjoying the soft feel of his mouth as he pushed kisses all over the top of her head.

"Jane, I must tell you about my father. He's the reason why I could never carry on a proper relationship with a woman. You see, he was stone cold to all of us and I had to watch my poor mother struggling to bring us up – my sister and I. "At an early age, I made a vow that I would never make a woman suffer the way my ma had to suffer – at least as soon as I understood what was going on. So I never had a girl for longer than a week or two and I couldn't discuss personal relationships with anybody. That is until I met you. But you would have to be married already, wouldn't you!

"However, the damage had already been done. I'd held myself back so many times before, that it became second nature and the guilt must have taken me over. That's why I had to run away. Oh Jane! Can you forgive me? Can we have another try at being close? When I left you and tried to carry on life without you, I saw your face in every flower, in every leaf on every tree. What I'm saying, Jane, is that I need you."

Jane had never expected to hear all this from any man. According to her experience, all men kept their feelings to themselves and never talked about anything so personal. Rob had poured out his heart to her; the words flowing like water from a hole in a river dam and she had a feeling that he would never expose his emotions so freely again. For Rob, this was the result of a lifetime of bitterness and unconscious protection for the women in his life. She must make him understand that he would never be like his father, never, with such an overflowing well of sensitivity. Only a totally uncaring and irresponsible person could treat his mate in such a callous fashion and Rob was not in the slightest way unfeeling.

She held his dear face in her hands and kissed his brow and then the end of his straight, tanned nose. There was something she had to say, and yet she dreaded spoiling this affectionate moment, when Rob had poured out his thoughts to her. But it had to be said. She was a married woman and she must make him understand that she would be his confidante but nothing more.

As a mother tunes in to the cries of her children, Jane heard a sound she recognised. The doorbell at the front of the house was clanging out into the garden, filtering through the open window. Her first impulse was to ignore it and then she remembered the boys up in their rooms. One of them would answer it and start searching for her.

"I must go, Rob. Oh, my dear, I don't want to but I must go before the boys find us. You stay here and I'll be back as soon as I can." He was smiling now, as she ran her fingers through her hair, trying to catch a glimpse of her reflection in the small window.

When she entered the back door, Henry was in the kitchen, just about to head for the back door.

"Mother. I wondered where you were. That man is at the door. You know, the one who came in for tea a while ago. The tall chap in the suit."

"Oh, you mean Mr Farquharson, the lawyer."

"Is that his name. I didn't know. Anyway, I've put him in the sitting room while I searched for you."

"Th…thank you, Henry," she said, wondering what she could tell Ken to encourage him to leave. He was sitting in his favourite chair, by the window, watching the birds in the lilacs and in the tall hedges on either side of the garden. As she entered, he stood up and came towards her, smiling.

"I hope you don't mind my turning up like this, Jane. I have been to see mother and thought I would take you up on your offer to call. Please say you have ten minutes to spare?"

How could she do this to Rob?

"Of course, Ken. How lovely to see you. How is your mother?"

"She's fine, just fine. She looks forward to my visits so much that I sometimes think I should move out here and commute into Edinburgh each day. That would be better for both of us," he said, a flirtatious look in his eyes. Oh no, not that. Jane was unsure how to handle such a situation. She must make it clear that she would not accept anything more than friendship, or perhaps not even that. Was she equipped to be rude to someone so nice.

"Oh, I believe it is very busy going into town in the mornings. My husband sometimes does it and often says…" This was the wrong thing to say. If Michael could do it, so could Ken.

"Well, it bears thinking about."

"A cup of tea, before you move on?"

"No thank you. I had one with my mother. I thought just a little chat, to lighten the day."

"I'm afraid I'm not the one to lighten your day." she said calmly. "As you can see, I have been busy in the garden and hardly like to sit down before taking a bath and getting changed."

"I am so sorry. I've caught you at a bad time. Maybe another occasion would be better," he said, starting to rise.

She was just about to lead him to the door, when she saw the front of Michael's car appear in the drive. As usual, he ground to a halt in front of the garage and marched around to the front entrance, rather than soil himself by walking through the kitchen. This was a situation she had not anticipated.

"Is that your husband, Jane? I must say hello before I go," Ken said, quite calmly.

Perhaps she had been imagining things when she thought he had shown an interest in her earlier.

The glass door at the front shut noisily and Michael walked straight into the room, almost knocking Ken over. Looking her up and down, without giving him a second glance, he glowered and said,

"What do you think you're doing in here in that revolting outfit. I know you play around in the kitchen and the garden looking like that – but in the sitting room!"

Jane ignored the comment and, smiling sweetly, said,

"Ken, this is my husband, Michael. Michael, Mr Kenneth Farquharson is just leaving. He wanted to stay and make your acquaintance before he went."

Ken held out his hand and said,

"How do you do, Mr Donaldson. I'm sure you know all about my legal conversations with your wife about her inheritance from Mrs Sanderson."

"No, I don't but I'm sure your business with my wife is over now. Pleased to meet you. Goodbye" and he opened the sitting room door wider, so that Ken could leave.

Goodbyes were said on the doorstep and Jane never once let her smile leave her face, as she waved him off. Ken exhibited an expression of puzzlement, as he said,

"I'll be in touch, Jane."

Going back to the sitting room, knowing that Rob was still in the summerhouse, was one of the most difficult things Jane had ever done. Little did she know that Ken's presence in the house was the best thing that could have happened.

"Right, madam! Why are you entertaining men in my house, in my absence and who in the Lord's name is Mr Farquharson? You've never mentioned him before. And as for your so-called inheritance from that mad bitch next door…"

"Please, keep your voice down. The boys are upstairs."

"What do I care! No doubt you and your boyfriend would be whispering sweet nothings if I hadn't come home from Glasgow early."

"Now you're being ridiculous."

"Ridiculous, is it? Am I supposed merely to accept the fact that you have a man in the house when I return? I don't find that ridiculous at all."

He raised his arm, as if to hit her and she ducked from habit. Feeling foolish as well as furious, Michael grabbed her arm and swung her towards him.

"Father! Stop that!" It was young Henry, standing in the doorway.

"Thank you, Henry," Jane said and wrenched herself away.

"It's alright, son. I wasn't going to hit her or anything. I just lost my temper."

"Don't give me that, Father. I know all about the arguments when you think we're asleep in bed. I don't know why I've put up with it for so long but it has to stop now. Do you hear me, Father. I'm not a child any more and I won't let you treat my mother this way!"

"Don't be silly, boy"

"I've spent enough nights sitting on the stairs, peering through the banisters, to know what you've been doing all these years. I'm just sorry I was such a coward and didn't try to stop you at the time."

"Oh, Henry," Jane said in a small, sad voice. She did not want to believe that her boy, her child, had woken up night after night and watched the farce that was her marriage. The whole reason for not leaving Michael before now was the children and now she had heard from Henry's own lips that he knew. Perhaps they both knew how their parents had behaved towards each other. It was time to make it better.

She recovered her equilibrium and faced Michael, in front of their son.

"That was the final straw, Michael. I have never criticised your behaviour, ever and, God knows, there has been plenty to criticise. I want you to know that I will be suing for divorce, as soon as possible and Henry is a witness to that!"

She clasped hold of Henry's hand and twirled the tall boy around to follow her out of the room and upstairs to his bedroom. Once there and with the door shut behind them, she said,

"Forgive me Henry. I would do anything to put the clock back so you didn't have to see that scene but you have seen it and I'm sorry but that is the end of our marriage."

"It alright, Mother. I understand, more than you realise. What I said about watching from the stairs is quite true and I've been doing it since I was a little tot. Seeing you arguing with father has put me clean off girls altogether, in case I turn out the same."

This was too much of a coincidence. Two men on the same day had confessed to being influenced by their fathers and she had been involved up to her neck in both occurrences. Rob! Rob! He must have left by now. He would surely have heard the cars on the drive. There was no way she could find out.

"Henry," she said quickly. "Listen to me. You are too loving and gentle to turn out anything like your father. If what you have seen has done anything for you, it is to make you behave in a totally opposite way and one day you will meet a girl who will make you realise that. Now, I must find out if Andrew heard any of that. Will you give me a few minutes to go to his room and find out?"

He nodded and she went up to Andrew's door, which was shut. She knocked, then entered, to find him lying flat out on his bed, surrounded by his possessions of bags, shoes, books and writing implements, snoring. Good, he had slept through the whole thing. What a relief. However, she would have to explain to him later why she was divorcing his father. Perhaps Henry would help her.

Back in Henry's tidy bedroom, the boy sat on the side of his bed, staring down at his black lace-up shoes and she knew she would have to continue their conversation, if only to allow him to talk about the dreadful prospect ahead of them.

"What are you thinking, darling?"

"Just what I told you, Mother, about not being keen on girls and, I feel at my age I should be."

This was good. He was more involved in his own feelings than what was happening to his parents.

"Do you know any girls?"

"Not really. I tend to avoid them as much as possible. Sometimes I see this girl at the bus stop and she said she's going up to university when I do. She's a proper nuisance – always wanting to chat, when all I want to do is catch a bus. She has a retriever dog and says she walks it in the woods."

Jane suddenly had a picture of a tall, dark-haired girl of about Henry's age, walking past the house and stopping to peer into the garden. She had even said hello once or twice before she walked on, past the house and then back to the main road.

"Why not offer to go with her next time?"

"Not likely. She might think I'm interested. Are you really going to leave him, Mother?" Their conversation was in bits and pieces.

"Yes, I'm afraid so, darling."

"Don't be afraid. This could be the answer for me. I could never imagine having friends and bringing them home to meet father. But now, or rather, soon – well it will all be different, won't it?"

"Yes, dear, totally different."

CHAPTER 31

Rob had left rapidly that day. No sooner had he heard the sound of Michael's car tyres on the gravel path, than he had grabbed his jacket and disappeared through a gap in the hedge, which led to Grace's old garden. Before he went, he left the sack of bulbs in the doorway of the summerhouse and arranged plant pots on top of the sea chest. No-one must know about their secret meeting place or indeed about Jane's little hideaway. As far as anyone else was concerned, it was a potting shed, used for just that.

000

The next time was so much easier; he decided to use his rat run from Grace's garden, the way he had left, to bring him straight into Jane's garden, rather than fool around knocking on doors and it was by far a better way – even though he felt ludicrous doing it. Luckily, the old house next door remained empty, waiting for a buyer. At least he could see Jane in the garden and ascertain whether she was alone, before coming through the hedge and she was always keen to see him.

"So much has changed since the last time, Rob. I've decided to sue for divorce because Henry caught Michael almost in the act of attacking me."

"No! Let me sort that man out for you. He can't be allowed to do such things. No man in his right mind would hit a woman."

"That's one of the problems. I don't think he is in his right mind."

She put her hand gently on Rob's mouth to stop any further outburst and he allowed her to continue. The idea of Jane being a free woman was one which threw him into a complicated mood. He had said he loved her but he still wanted to retain his own freedom. He hoped she would not get thoughts of marriage into her head because he needed time to think all this out. Being able to talk to her about his childhood had certainly helped but it would take some time before he felt able to act on his new thoughts. Maybe in six months or a year's time he would feel more like putting down roots. And no doubt it would take some time for her to get the wheels of divorce in action.

Jane was still talking and he had not heard a word. "When the doorbell rang the other day, it was Ken Farquharson, the lawyer who dealt with old Grace's estate and Michael thought I had been entertaining him, whilst all the time you were down here in the summerhouse. I told him there and then that I was going to leave him. You see the boys know all about his furies and his regular verbal attacks on me at night. At least Henry does and I suppose he's told Andrew. An idea came to me in the middle of the night. I'm going to need a lawyer and I already have a tame one turning up on my doorstep, Mr Farquarson who is dealing with Grace's will.

"The other thing I desperately wanted to tell you yesterday is this. And I do hope it won't upset you. I feel very forward about saying something so personal. But I must get my thoughts out, just as you did."

Rob was sitting, looking most perplexed and somewhat like a wild animal, just about to take flight. So Jane felt she must put him out of his misery. Or perhaps she was putting him right into some misery.

"Rob, we must never let our friendliness and affection become any more than it is. I love you as a friend and will always do so. But I am not the kind of woman who embarks upon affaires. And never will be. I am still a married woman and my sons trust me to be the guiding light in their lives. If you and I became more than friends, I would hurt them more than you will ever know." She stopped, took several deep breaths, then had the courage to look at Rob. He was looking down at the floor and only looked up because she had stopped her tirade.

"Jane, you have nothing to fear from me. Nor have you a reason to think that I would force you into a relationship we could not pursue out in the open. I feel as you feel, that our time together is sacred; we are good friends, nothing more."

Jane held out her hand and Rob clasped it; then he did the best thing he could do in the circumstances. He kissed her fingertips, in the old chivalrous fashion.

Now Jane could tell him the next important reason for wanting to see him. Something which made her proud and fearful at the same time.

"Rob, Andrew has joined the Navy. That's why I think he knows all about his father."

"What! That is a surprise."

"I can't say I find it surprising myself. I told you how introverted he's been since coming back from BB camp. Seemingly he had the idea in his mind from that day and he's been mulling it over ever since. He went off to Edinburgh, to the Recruiting Office, yesterday. He's going up north to do his training at the beginning of September."

"That's only a few weeks. And didn't you say Henry starts university at the end of September as well?"

"Yes, I'll be all alone soon but I intend to find a little cottage in Uphall when Michael and I start talking again and I can explain to him what I'm doing. By the end of the year, you might have a new neighbour." She was trying to make a joke out of her move from the mansion to a small place in the village where Rob lived. But he took her comment seriously and said,

"Don't scoff, young lady. I happen to know there's a cottage in the same row as mine, which is coming up for sale shortly. Would you like me to make enquiries for you?"

Jane thought this was incredible and seemed too good to be true. She might end up living very close to Rob and it would be worse than it was now. How could they slip in and out of each others' houses, when he knew everyone around him? She was unsure.

"I don't know Rob. People tend to talk."

"Let them," he said firmly, now sure he had made the right decision.

Jane wondered if he was planning anything more permanent, regardless of what she had just said and, if so, she would have to inform him again that she was not ready for more than they already had. Thoughts of frying pans and fires leapt into her mind. But it was nothing like that, was it?

"It's likely to be a long time before I'm ready to move. It will do no harm to investigate but please, no names."

Rob left soon after and Jane stayed on the sea chest for some time, writing her journal, because she had so much to explain about losing her beloved house and her hated husband. The sun went down over the conifers, leaving dark shadows across the lawn and birds flew around noisily, returning to their nests which had almost outlived their usefulness, most of the chicks having flown. She now had to become accustomed to her own chicks flying the nest and it was not an easy situation, particularly as she was about to fly away as well. How miserable it would be, leaving this lovely old house on which she had lavished so much attention. All her tenderness had been manifested in hand-sewn cushions, all her affection exhibited in cakes and pies created in her kitchen refuge; it was time to move on. If she and Rob did not come together as a couple, she would have a new home on which to lavish her attention. Yes, it was the right thing to do.

The following day, Andrew asked if he could have a quiet word with her. She was so unaccustomed to her younger son needing a shoulder to cry on that she was flippant as she said,

"Of course, my dear boy. No doubt you want to discuss vests and socks for the Navy. It will be a little different from the Boys' Brigade, I expect."

"It's nothing to do with my smalls, Mother. I only wish it were that simple. I won't beat about the bush. I'll come straight to the point."

This sounded ominous.

"When I went to Boys' Brigade, I met a girl, a girl I really liked and I wanted to see more of her. I found out where she lives and I went round and asked her to come out with me but she turned me down. Believe it or not, she said she was too young to have a permanent boyfriend and more or less shut the door in my face. I was so upset that day, that I went into Edinburgh and joined up. That's why I did it."

"I can't believe what I'm hearing. You mean you only enlisted because of your first girlfriend? Or should I say your first non-girfriend. That was very childish, Andrew."

"I know, Mum. But now I've had time to think and I know I'll make a go of it. Now I can say I've joined up for the right personal reasons."

Jane was speechless. What did he expect her to say? She left him sitting at the kitchen table and rushed off to her bedroom. This was dreadful. Only one good thing had come out of this tragic little situation. She had always assured the boys they could tell her anything and Andrew had done just that. It must have been a nightmare for him, plucking up the courage to explain his silly behaviour. To join the armed forces on a whim was worse than being a conscientious objector.

She crossed the room to the door, then went back and straightened the coverlet on her bed, thinking this out. She must have a serious five minutes before re-approaching Andrew. So, she sat on the low nursing chair and closed her eyes. As she allowed her mind to ramble, she realised that her own actions in divorcing Michael could never affect a sailor at sea, nor could it ruin the life of a university student, living away from home. Everything worked out for the best, eventually.

Andrew was still sitting at the kitchen table, his face in his hands now, when she returned. She cleared her throat and said,

"It's alright, my son. I can understand what happened to you. But as you get older you will realise that it's much better to sleep on a decision, rather than charge off and do the first thing that comes into your head."

Jane was speaking from personal experience because she had thought and thought before finally telling Michael she was going to leave him.

CHAPTER 32

That lovely girl, Stephanie, came to see Jane several days later. She introduced herself and explained that she was a friend of Andrew's. It was lucky that Jane had had the conversation with her son, so she knew who this girl was. And what a pretty young thing she was. As she walked into the house, wearing a worried frown, it was obvious that she had spent hours thinking about this meeting. Why she had come, was yet to be revealed.

"Hello, my dear. Come and sit down," Jane said, in a friendly manner, despite her inner feelings. She wanted this girl to see her as someone who could help her and not as an ogre, the unhelpful mother of the man who did not intend to take her out. Because that was what this complicated charade was all about. She wanted to hear some truths from this sad little mouth before she dropped her own private shell. However, Stephanie had some ideas of her own. She pressed her mouth into a determined line and, sitting on the edge of the settee, she said,

"Mrs Donaldson, I hope you don't mind me coming to see you. You see, I was very rude to Andrew when he came to ask me to go out with him and I've just heard from one of his friends that he's joined the Navy. I just want to make sure it's nothing to do with me, that's all. When we talked at West Barnes, he said nothing about joining up ..." She ran out of steam and took out her hanky to wipe her eyes.

Good, she knew what Andrew was going to do. So there would be no need to tell her. And it was good that Andrew had thought out his reasons for going into the Navy, which he said was now nothing to do with Stephanie. Although Jane wasn't quite sure about that.

"Slow down, slow down", she said. "You sound just like Andrew when he explained to me why he was leaving. You can rest assured that he's joined the Navy for his own reasons and it was nothing to do with you." Jane crossed her fingers because she had told a big lie. She had only told this fine girl the last part of Andrew's conversation.

"Oh, I'm so glad about that, Mrs Donaldson. You see I've been losing sleep about turning him down so crossly and if I thought he had gone off to sea, rather than see me again ... You see, the thing is, I like him a lot and would love to go out with him but I've got a very strict father and he stands guard over me whenever I go out and waits for me coming home, so he can smell my breath and check my lipstick's still on. You see I'm only sixteen and he feels a girl should be a lot older before she starts dating boys."

This put a whole new perspective on Andrew's problem. This girl liked him as much as he liked her. But nothing could be done about it now. They were both so young. There would be others for each of them. But it was important enough for Stephanie to come round and speak to her when Andrew was out. She felt such sympathy for both of them.

"Stephanie, I quite understand what you must be going through. But Andrew will be a sailor very soon and I feel you must try to put him out of your mind. You are too young to become so keen on one boyfriend. When you are older you will understand." She kept saying this 'when you are older' thing and yet – she was older and did she completely understand the workings of her own emotions.

The girl bowed her head, then stood up to go. "Thank you for listening, Mrs Donaldson. You see I have no-one to talk to about such things."

"What about your own mother, my dear?"

"We don't talk much; she's out a lot." There was no need to tell this kind lady that her mum had a job in the local pub and spent most of her time there, coming home the worse for wear at the end of the night and sleeping until lunchtime the next day.

Jane felt sorry for the child, because that's all she was, a child dressed up in adult clothing. Perhaps she could become a surrogate mother to her. Here she went again, planning to mother somebody else. All she wanted in life was to be needed and her two sons were flying the nest, so what better than to nurture this girl. But perhaps Stephanie did not need a shoulder to cry on or an older woman with whom to share her worries?

CHAPTER 33

War was declared while Andrew was doing his training. He knew there was trouble brewing when he joined up but had not expected this. Hitler had invaded Poland and France, and Neville Chamberlain, The Prime Minister, had broadcast on the radio that Britain was at war with Germany. He wondered how people in London had felt when they heard their first trial air-raid warning.

The Royal Navy was scheduled to take the British Expeditionary Force to France and then to blockade European waterways against the German fleet. It was said that blockades were what won wars, by depriving the enemy of food and other necessities and Andrew remembered hearing stories of how the German people had been starved in this way during the Great War, previously.

He was nineteen now and felt he was a man. If there was any way he could get into this war, he had been determined to take it But he was informed by officers and naval ratings alike that the only way to get out of training quickly and onto a proper ship was to listen to instructors and obey, obey, obey. And although it went against every thought in his head he did. And by May, 1940 he was on board a destroyer.

000

The cottage which was for sale beside Rob, in Uphall, was ideal for Jane and she was to move in shortly after Andrew left. Henry would come with her but it was only for weeks because he had found rooms in Halls of Residence near to his college and intended moving in before term started, with the help of Rob and his large van.

Jane had asked Stephanie if she would like to come to visit her when Andrew went away. She had mentioned to her son that she had spoken to Stephanie and that the girl did like him, although her father felt she was too young to take him up on his offer to take her out. She felt that Andrew was happier knowing that he had not been ignored deliberately and he merely said, laughingly,

"Oh well, perhaps I'll pick up where we left off, when I get home in a few years' time."

He was making a joke out of the situation now, so he must have accepted how things were. The chances were that he would meet a girl in every port, as sailors were meant to, and the name Stephanie would hardly be remembered the next time he came home on leave.

So, he went off for his training with a free mind, not worrying that the first girl he had fancied did really like him and her refusal was nothing personal. Fathers could be so annoying to the younger generation and tended to treat daughters like little girls, long after they had grown up.

However, Stephanie did come to see Jane on a regular basis, enjoying the company of an older woman who would listen to her little problems, because her mother wouldn't. Then when war broke out, and Andrew had left training camp, Jane started to worry that he would be in the thick of things before long.

It was a pity his mother had no other woman on which to inflict her own problems; Stephanie was too young and too involved for her to even breathe a hint of Andrew's potential assignments.

One day, Jane was packing up her personal belongings, prior to moving house to the cottage beside Rob, when Stephanie rang the front door bell. Jane wiped her hands on her apron and walked down the hall, which was strewn with boxes, ready to be taken away by Rob in his van. It was good to see her young friend on the doorstep and her presence reminded Jane of the many times she had stood in the same position at the house next door, to visit Grace.

"Hello, my dear. It's lovely to see you. Come along in," she said.

"Thanks Jane. I'm only here for a short time. I can see you're up to the eyes in packing. Would you like some help?" she asked as an afterthought.

"No thank you, Stephanie but it's kind of you to ask. Come and sit in the kitchen and we'll have the proverbial nice cup of tea."

"That would be fine and it will give me a chance to tell you my news."

This sounded interesting. So, after the kettle had puffed out steam in the large old kitchen, they sat at the long pine table, cups of tea in front of them and an open box of biscuits unceremoniously beside them. If Michael had seen this in the earlier days, he would have raised the roof. But now it hardly mattered what he saw and he had prevented himself from commenting on anything Jane did now she was deserting him, as he liked to describe her going.

"Now, my young friend. Tell me all your news. This must be something quite important for you to walk all this way, just for a short visit."

"Yes, it's probably the most important thing I've done in my whole life," she said, smiling, Then she took a bite of biscuit, so Jane had to wait until her mouth was empty, to hear the momentous news. But it was well worth the wait. "I've joined up, Jane," she said.

Jane had a distinct feeling of deja vous. This was not only uncanny but it was almost as disappointing as the first time she had heard those words from her son. How could she look as if she felt pleased?

"Joined up? Whatever made you do that? I would have thought you were too young to enlist."

"Having an honest face helps. I just told a little fib about my age. And they're so keen to get anyone into the services that it worked a treat," she said. "By the time they receive my birth certificate I could be in the middle of training – and they're hardly likely to send me home to add another year onto my age, are they?"

"I suppose not," Jane said, quietly. Then, remembering that this was not another of her offspring, she asked the obvious question. "What do your parents feel about this?"

"Not much, by their attitude. Mum just grinned and wished me luck, as if I was going in for an exam at school. Dad said it would be the making of me, surprising me to bits."

"You mean he was all for it? What happened to his guard-dog mentality? I suppose he doesn't know how many servicemen are in the army."

"Oh, I haven't joined the army, Jane. I've gone into the Senior Service, as a radio operator."

Jane could have been knocked down with the proverbial feather. This was history repeating itself indeed. "Why?" she asked, dreading the answer.

"Because I did my homework and realised that I could be more useful sitting in front of a desk, helping the armed forces, than sitting in front of a desk, studying. Before you mention it, there was not a tiddly-tiny thought of Andrew in my head at the time." Then she started to laugh and Jane had to join in.

Jane flung her arms round the cheerful girl, then handed out the biscuits again and topped up their cups of tea.

"This calls for a celebration," she said, holding her cup aloft. Stephanie did the same and they toasted Stephanie's forthcoming venture in very strong tea.

000

In the North Sea, on board a cruiser, where he had been transferred from his destroyer, Andrew lay in his hammock and reread the letter, for the umpteenth time. Mum said Stephanie had joined the Navy, as a radio operator. That was so weird. Of course girls never went to sea and men needed all the help they could get from land-locked staff. Perhaps she would pass on important messages to his ship. And he would never know. He still thought about the lovely girl he had seen on the beach at West Barnes and often wondered if her dad had let her out of the house yet. But here she was going off to a naval base, all by herself. No doubt all the guys would be after her now.

"Whatchu doing in there, Andy? I thought you was on for a game of cards," his Irish mate said, rocking his hammock so he almost fell out.

"OK, OK. I'm coming."

"She must be quite something, your girl. You never stop reading her letters."

He refused to admit that he was reading a letter from his mother. That would put him in line for too much lip, from the likes of him and his pals, so he just grinned and let it pass.

They were sitting on board ship, guarding the exit to the Atlantic, where a line of cruisers had been stationed to inspect unknown vessels for contraband. Great Britain had produced many new ships in the 1930s, of the battleship and cruiser classes, whereas Germany could only boast of building half a dozen during the same period. So the men on Andrew's ship and others in the fleet felt there were enough in each convoy to frighten off any enemy fighting vessels, with their guns fore and aft, not to mention their own 'secret enemy', their torpedoes. Andrew had trained as a gunner so these features were nearest to his heart. They also always mustered a boarding party who made decisions as to whether contraband goods would be sent on to a British port or allowed to continue on to a neutral country. It had been quiet so far and none of his rigorous training had been of use. A bit like hanging around a street corner, waiting for a rival gang to appear. It had been rumoured that blockades would be made total as soon as other European countries were allied to Britain for the duration of the war. There was still the possibility that Germany would bring materials from Japan in their recently thrown-together U-boats. These submarines were the bane of the Royal Navy because they were capable of sinking any warships with very little warning. In fact, after The Great War, it had been declared illegal by the Treaty of Versailles for Germany to build the things but they seemed to be going great guns to produce as many as they could for this war.

As Andrew made his way to the mess, after hiding away his precious letter, he tried not to see the bleakness all around him. Admittedly, it was clean. Petty Officer saw to that, with his rigorous inspections, even in the middle of war, and it was a common sight to see the bottoms of ratings wagging around as they scrubbed the decks and anything else liable to become sullied by the feet of the men. Nobody wanted to be on deck duty but it was a good way of making friends; who could refuse to have a natter when there was nothing else to do but push a scrubbing brush from one end of the ship to the other?

There was a group gathered around one of the deal tables, perched on stools which he was sure had been invented for their lack of comfort. He would have to be quick because card schools were frowned upon and it was quite possible that it would only last a short time.

CHAPTER 34

Henry slumped in a broken-down old armchair in his digs, looking at the well-known scribble on the letter in front of him. How many books had been ruined for him by this spider's web of so-called writing during his childhood? He had owned 'A Child's Garden of Verses' by Robert Louis Stevenson and loved the complicated black and white drawings which accompanied each verse, particularly that of the poem called 'Windy Nights' of a long-haired man with bare legs riding a wild horse. Andrew had not only added his own ending to the rhyme but had coloured-in jodhpurs and boots in a sickly pink crayon. He could never read it now without thinking of his brother's silly, invented final verse:

'Whenever my brother's crying aloud,
For his mother to come and see.
By on the staircase, low and loud,
By at the gallop goes he;
Off to the lavvy he goes and then,
By he comes back at the gallop again.'

He knew Henry was frightened of the dark and laughed about it, even to the point of making up doggerel. Now Andrew's messy writing had come from the middle of the sea somewhere. There was no need to wonder about the identification of the ship, or even what type it was because all that was missing from the letter, according to Government ruling.

As he started to decipher the front page, Henry realised that he was the only member of the family receiving a missive from Andrew. He was being asked to keep it dark about hearing from his brother and also to send him information about that young girl, Stephanie, if his mother told him anything. This was a laugh. When Andrew had joined up, he had said he wanted nothing more to do with Stephanie. Now he wanted detailed information about everything. He said he had received a letter from mother, telling him a bit about her joining up. But he knew Henry went home some weekends and he might know more. His young brother must be home-sick.

Henry was enjoying his course and student life. Being a quiet person, he preferred to closet himself in his room with a pile of books, rather than hit the high spots but he was not averse to a quiet drink at the pub, or a chat with other chaps on his floor.

Since he had started university, he had seen something of Margaret, the girl from Uphall whom he met sometimes in the refectory. She was another serious, quiet type, which made it doubly difficult for them to get to know each other, not that he wanted to, but he had to say something, when she appeared at his table. He had probably asked her about her dog every time they met!

000

Jane had also spoken to Margaret, now that she knew she was an acquaintance of Henry's at university and due to the fact that she now lived on the route taken by many dog-walking people to a path along the burn. There was a thin line between being friendly and being nosy, so she determined not to mention anything personal, keeping all conversation to the garden and walks around the area and never mentioning Henry, apart from saying he had talked about her going up to university.

The girl came home more frequently than Henry did, which was not difficult because Jane had only seen him twice since the beginning of term, and she obviously loved walking her parents' dog whenever she could. Now, all conversations obviously centred on the war and how little it affected people in Scotland and Jane was loathe to join in, just in case she had to mention Andrew. As far as she was concerned, he was abroad in the Navy but not being sure whether she would ever see him again made her reluctant even to speak his name. He had never replied to her letter, so he probably never got it or did not care two hoots about her.

One day, Margaret stopped to chat, just about black-out curtains and digging for Britain, allowing the dog to sniff around while she leant on the garden gate. The quiet girl was a bit more forthcoming these days, having come to know Jane better.

What a pleasant girl. She wondered how much Henry saw of her at university and whether they were actually friends. She had a charming manner and seemed so easy to talk to, now she had got to know her. That was the kind of friend he needed

000

Next time Margaret saw Henry sitting by himself at a table in the hall, munching attentively at a Digestive biscuit, she went over and asked whether anybody was sitting there. Henry always thought that was a ridiculous thing to say; obviously no-one was sitting there, unless it was The Invisible Man but, rather than make a sarcastic quip, he merely shook his head. For a while he had thought she liked him but recently they had only waved from a distance. A good-looking girl like that must have lots of boyfriends.

"Do you mind if I join you, Henry? I feel we have something in common."

What on earth could they have in common? But he motioned towards the vacant chair and Margaret left her jacket and went off to get her lunch.

He was dying of curiosity the whole time she stood in the queue, so that he had finished his biscuit and was quietly slurping his cup of coffee with a welcoming smile, when she reappeared. She was wearing one of those jumpers called Sloppy Joes and it came down almost to her knees, leaving a bit of pleated skirt showing a bit lower down. Unfortunately, she seemed to think she had to paint up her face with bright red lipstick and blue stuff on her eyelids. Why didn't girls live with the faces they had been given?

"I can't think what we have in common, Margaret, apart from the fact that we both come from Uphall. And we've done that subject to death."

She was glad to be talking like real friends at last and said, "I met your mother when I went home last weekend. She was in the garden and I stopped and had quite a chat. What a lovely person she is."

"Yes," said Henry, disappointed that the item they had in common was his mother.

"Don't tell me you don't love her a lot. You couldn't help it. I believe your brother's away in the Navy."

"If you want the truth, I've only been back twice since I started here."

"Oh Henry! How could you do that? She must miss you."

"It's easy. I just get so involved in my studies."

"I'll bet even your brother's been home more often than you."

"Believe it or not, he hasn't been back on leave since he was posted. He's on a ship somewhere secret."

Due to Henry's couldn't care less manner, Margaret thought the conversation was at an end and planned to move on now that her lunch was over but Henry suddenly looked at her with a wistful expression and said,

"I don't suppose you're going back to the sticks this weekend, are you?"

"Yes. I usually try to pop out there, most weekends, to see my parents."

"What a good daughter!" he said and smiled sarcastically. But it was true. She was a good daughter. And he was an abominable son, wasn't he?

"Daughters are usually better than sons at that kind of thing, haven't you noticed?"

She said this without a trace of sarcasm. She really meant it. So he decided to be his normal straightforward self, instead of trying to be a clever clogs.

"Can't say I have. I don't know many daughters."

His face had gone pensive again, so Margaret said,

"Why did you ask me if I would be going home?"

"Oh, nothing," he said a bit too casually. "I just wondered if you would mind if I joined you on your walk with the dog, as I happen to be going home this weekend." There, he'd done it.

Margaret wanted to say something flippant like, 'surprise surprise' but knew it would be the wrong thing to do. Henry was not the kind of boy you fooled around with. He had obviously been reminded that he had not seen his mother much since the beginning of term and wanted to put it right. If she had been the catalyst that made him remember, then she was glad. His mother was a nice woman.

"Lovely. I would enjoy that," she said. "When shall we meet – Sunday?"

"What about Saturday afternoon. I'll look out for you."

So that's how it felt, making a date with a girl, Henry thought. It wasn't as difficult as he'd imagined. Going for a walk in the countryside was a good thing to do because you could always say you'd had enough walking and cut the meeting short if it all got too much on the day.

He went off to his tutorial with a smile on his face and a twinkle in his eye. None of his friends could believe it was the same chap; they were so used to his serious nature and sensible conversation. Not that he was not popular, because he was. His love of sport and his knowledge about Rugby football were enough to make him one of the most sought-after men in the classes. Any time there was an argument to be decided on the name of a player or the date of a certain game, Henry was the one who knew, so he was forever in demand.

He decided to go home after morning studies on Friday, so that he could make his peace with his mother, without anyone else around. He also felt that he should warn her in advance that he would be gone for most of Saturday afternoon, in case she wanted to organise an outing or somesuch. So he just threw a few things into an old sports bag and caught a bus in the centre of Edinburgh.

The war had not changed Edinburgh much, apart from the anxious looks on the faces of people passing by and the fact that everyone wanted to chat in shops or at the bus stops. There was nothing like common consternation for bringing out the patriotism and fraternity in people. But people still walked along Princes Street and sat in the gardens, the women wore fine hats and men carried silver-topped walking sticks. It was still the capital of Scotland and, from the conversations he heard, the citizens were not going to let a mere painter like Adolf Hitler alter their haughty enjoyment of their city or their arrogant behaviour.

After a quiet journey, the bus drew up in Uphall village, at the Post Office and Henry noted with pleasure the date above the old stone building of 1890. This was the first time he had even considered local history but he knew from his mother that this line of sandstone houses and shops next to the old inn had been built for the shale oil workers in the days when Uphall was deemed to be the industrial capital of the area. How could a small place like this glory in the title, 'the biggest village in Scotland'? He climbed down the steps and waved to the driver as the bus drove on to Bathgate.

His mother's cottage was behind the main street and Henry had lived there for such a short time that he had to struggle to remember exactly where it was. However, there were several clues, such as the winding path which led over the burn and through a few trees and soon he was opening a little wooden gate leading to this oh-so-small house. His mother must really have had to talk herself into living in such a tiny space, compared with their big house in Ecclesmachan. He expected his father was still there but he did not anticipate finding out because communication had fizzled out between them.

As he opened the squeaky garden gate, he wondered how his mother would welcome him, or not, maybe.

CHAPTER 35

Henry's weekend started well. He knocked on his own front door and, surprisingly, it was opened by Rob, the man whose company he had enjoyed at Ecclesmachan. If it had not been for his mother and her determination that he should attend university, he could well have become a gardener and part-time philosopher like Rob because he found everything about the job relaxing.

"Hello, my friend! Please excuse me for answering your mother's door, as if I lived here, which I don't."

Henry liked his attitude to life. He'd got that straight out into the open, instead of blushing and blustering. Nothing seemed to worry Rob. But he said that far too quickly, didn't he? Was there anything going on between those two?

"Don't worry about that, Rob. I'm pleased to see you, at last. It must be ages since we met." Keep it simple, that was the way to play it.

"Yes but now that your mother and I are neighbours I often drop in for a cup of tea and a chat. You must come round to my place and I'll show you my little garden. Oh, I hear the footsteps of your ma."

An inside door opened and there she stood. When Jane saw who it was, he thought she was going to fling her drying-up cloth in his face but she remembered just in time and said a hurried, 'excuse me darling I won't be a second', while she raced into the scullery with it, flinging it onto the rack.

"Oh Henry, I'm so glad to see you," she said, when she reappeared.

"Yes, I was just telling Henry he must come and look at the garden and tell me what he thinks of it."

Henry thought this was strange. They were like a newly married couple and yet Henry knew his mother must be well into her forties and Rob a bit older. It was like visiting the house of a young woman and her husband, not a bit like the way it was with his father, although Rob had made it clear that they didn't live together. They must have some kind of agreement.

He should have come home before now and experienced the friendly, homely atmosphere of this cottage.

Rob said his fond farewells and went off down the street, with a wave as he passed the window and Henry sat down on his empty chair, at his mother's insistence, while she went into the kitchen and made some food. The fire crackled in the grate and there was the well-remembered noise of clattering crockery harking from the next room. Why hadn't he done this before? There was so much loving comfort here.

ooo

On Saturday afternoon, Margaret walked down the road with Ben the dog and this time she lifted the catch on the gate and went on down the garden path to the little front door. Henry was going to come with her for a walk. Her eyes were attracted by the riot of collapsed, colourful, cottage garden flowers and several overgrown shrubs, which looked pleasant enough from the gate but cried out for a gardener's hand to put them into order when inspected at close quarters. She saw some activity at the window, before she reached the green, panelled door, and suddenly it was flung open and out jumped Henry. He was holding a trowel in one hand and a bucket in the other and obviously didn't expect anyone to be there. It looked as if he had been weeding and just popped back into the house for something, his tools still in his hands.

"I thought you liked a bit of peace when you came home?" she said and thought how well he suited the role of gardener.

"I also like a bit of fun," he said, smiling more than she had ever seen him smile before.

As Henry had warned his mother that she was not to appear and offer that famous 'nice cup of tea', she was conspicuous by her absence and only the flicker of a bedroom curtain gave the lie to the fib that Henry had told – his mother was out shopping. So he grabbed his jacket from a peg and off they went, Ben sniffing him all over, as if to commit him to memory.

Their walk took them along the burn and over several fields, some of stubble left behind when the corn was cut and one of short grass where hay had been harvested. The dog happily sniffed long-gone rabbits and foxes, weaving in and out of long grasses on the sides of the meadows and the two friends walked on, at marching pace, until they reached the fenced-off area which marked the line of the railway.

"This looks like a natural turning point, to me," Henry said.

"It looks like a natural escape to me," Margaret answered.

"Now what do you mean by saying that? Why-ever would you want to escape – and where would you go?"

"It was a flippant comment about something incredibly serious. For years I have lived in this small corner of the world and I've never seen any of the exciting cities of Europe, nor those of America and beyond. When I was a child, I always saw a railway or a long, straight road as a means of escape from West Lothian."

"Well, this railway was never built as an escape to anywhere. When it was first put down by Irish navvies who lived in the rows of cottages at Uphall Station and other local villages, it was made to ferry the shale to the refinery at Pumpherston, so it could be turned into oil. However, it takes regular passengers from Edinburgh to Glasgow now. But of course you know that already, I expect."

"Who, in this neck of the woods doesn't. I wonder how many people of our age-group had a father or uncle, who worked down the mines. Hundreds or maybe thousands I would think. I know mine did. What about yours?"

"Mine is a member of the hierarchy, the ones who told everybody else what to do. When he started working at Middleton Hall, in the laboratories, my mother told me he looked down on everyone he knew."

"Surely not, they were all in the same business – making oil to sell around the world, to earn money to keep their families."

"Try telling my father that. You would think he was personally in charge of the whole thing. The day my mother moved out was the best day in my life."

"Why was that, Henry?" Margaret couldn't believe anyone would say such a cruel thing about their own father. Then she found out why.

"Because he constantly put me down and made me feel unworthy. I worked hard to go to university and he didn't say a word of encouragement at all. I'm amazed that he still finances my education but I suppose the thought of my telling my cronies that I had to leave for monetary reasons would be more than he could bear. In other words, I'm still studying because my father's a snob. Luckily, my mother's the opposite."

"I didn't realise you'd had a tough life before university. I was lucky to have two parents who loved each other and translated the same feeling to their six children. Unfortunately, with such a big family and such a small house, we were all forced to move out as quickly as we could. I was the brainy one, so I was sent to college, even though I fought against the fact that I was different, by wearing lots of make-up and trying to dress in up-to-the-minute fashions given to me by aunties. I honestly don't know how my parents can afford to keep me there, so I feel I have to do well to make them proud of me."

"And you will. I know you will." Now he knew about the make-up. And he knew quite a lot more about this girl and why she worked so hard. She was just his kind of person.

Henry took hold of her hand, as they turned to go back the way they had come. He was feeling incredibly brave because she relaxed him, almost the way his mother did. A steaming train came into view and, as it chugged away up the track, Margaret lifted her other hand and waved to the passengers.

She laughed and said, "That's what we used to do, when my dad took us for a walk, all six of us under the age of twelve. I can remember picking big laurel leaves and writing words with our fingernails. It was known as invisible writing and stayed that way until warmed up in a pocket next to your body, when it would appear as if by magic in brown letters on the green leaves."

"What good fun."

"It was. Most of life was fun and now we're all over the country."

She sounded sad and Henry squeezed her hand gently, putting it into his own pocket for warmth. This small act of affection made Margaret turn her head and kiss him gently on his cheek. She knew she had found someone who could sympathise with her about feelings and relationships at last.

Suddenly, she pulled her hand out of his pocket and started to look around, panic-stricken.

"Wh...what's wrong. Was it something I said?" Henry stammered, thinking he had put his foot in it again.

"It's Ben! Where is he? We've been talking away and I completely forgot about the dog. Ben! Ben!" she shouted.

Henry joined in and gave several loud whistles through his fingers but there was no answering rustle in the bushes or appearance of a leaping dog.

"We should retrace our footsteps, to see if he found a good place to sniff when we stopped at the fence. Oh, my God, I've just realised how near it was to the railway line and the bars of the fence were not exactly close together!"

"Don't worry, Margaret. We'll find him." Henry grabbed her hand again and they both ran off down the muddy path, slipping and sliding as they went. They passed a man also walking his dog and shouted at him, 'Have you seen a golden retriever. We've lost him!"

"Aye, lad. I saw one down by the railway fence a minute ago." Then he turned and walked off with his little Cairn terrier.

"We're almost there. Don't worry. Give him another shout."

"Ben! Ben!" Margaret yelled hoarsely. Then they saw him. He had climbed through the metal slats and was walking along the railway line, quite calmly sniffing the ground between the sleepers.

"Oh no! What if a train comes? What shall we do?"

"Leave it to me," Henry said, in the way of all heroes in films. Then he heard a chugging sound in the distance. What Margaret had dreaded was about to happen. Without another word, Henry left her side and ran at top speed to the fence, quickly climbed up it and jumped off the top bar. There was no time for thinking because the train was coming closer and closer. Luckily Ben had stopped to investigate and Henry rushed forward onto the line, grabbing the dog's leather collar as he did so. It was less than a minute before the train covered the area where they had stood and rattled on, while both Henry and dog pulled themselves out of the grassy ditch on the other side of the line. There was a loud scream and Henry heard his name yelled out, over the noise of the steam train. He took a firmer hold on Ben's collar and shouted back,

"It alright, Margaret! We're both safe!" As he finished the sentence the cloud of steam lifted and they could see each other across the track. She had her hand over her mouth, her eyes above looking large and terrified; he held the dog by the collar and wore a smile which felt half a mile wide.

CHAPTER 36

"I think it's all going well for Henry," Jane told Rob, as they pulled out unwanted plants in her front garden. "He seems to have developed a real liking for young Margaret; you know, the girl from Uphall at his college."

"That's good to hear. Now, what about Andrew? Have you heard from him?"

"Not a word and I know there's plenty of trouble at sea. I listen to the radio constantly but it's all doom and gloom regarding our boys, regardless of the fact that they predicted a turn in fortunes for the navy, now that the Bismarck has been sunk. Thank goodness we have Churchill as Prime Minister. He's a tonic for us all. But I keep thinking of my brave son on board ship and wondering if anyone would even tell me if he were blown up or drowned."

"I expect he's arranged all that. He would, you know, when he went to war. There's a deep love in every man for his mother and he wouldn't leave you in ignorance, should he ... if he had the slightest idea that he could be killed. The best thing you can do is forget all these pessimistic thoughts and tell yourself that one day he'll walk through the door and give you a hug."

"How wonderful that would be. But I think I've lost him forever."

They carried on working until a huge cloud covered the sky and they felt a few drops of the forecast rain. Then they went in for a cup of reviving tea.

Rob saw an opportunity for serious talk and turned to Jane as they sat together on the settee.

"You've been in this cottage for a while now and your divorce was settled months ago. I expect you're wondering why I haven't proposed to you?"

This was Rob to a T. No messing around. He just said it as he felt it.

"No, not at all," Jane said flippantly, trying very hard not to sound interested in the subject at all.

"Oh, don't get me wrong." Rob said. "I'm very fond of you. I love you dearly. You know that but I'm of the opinion that we need some time before making commitments. I just thought we should bring the subject out into the open, in case you were desperate to be married again."

"It's so soon after my divorce that I really hadn't given it a thought," she said, hoping her words sounded carefree and casual.

"That's what I thought you would say. A second marriage would be a big step for you. Everything is hunky-dory the way it is. We live next door to each other, so you always know where to go if anything goes wrong."

"Yes, Rob, everything's fine." Hunky-dory even, if she knew what this strange expression meant. How could she possibly reiterate her thoughts that they should continue to be good friends forever, when he had now forgotten all they had said in the summerhouse.

000

Andrew's ship, being a cruiser and therefore much in demand as an escort ship for the larger battleships, seemed to have led a charmed life. She had narrowly escaped any bombardments and avoided being blasted by shore attacks when reconnoitering enemy territory. Each man on board had his own talisman, which he was convinced had protected him throughout the first few years of this hellish war. Andrew carried a soiled brown penny which Stephanie had dropped that fateful day, which he held in his trouser pocket whenever things got rough. He was surprised the date and the king's head were still legible, the number of times he had rubbed it between his thumb and forefinger. But it was probably because she was the only girl he knew ashore and he didn't want to be left out of this talisman thing.

They were due to take part in a transfer of troops to the channel ports of France for a mission in the early part of the year and spirits were high. Their speed and knowledge of the coastline were in their favour and, despite only carrying six-inch guns, they were determined to succeed. Andrew's guns were his children and he checked them over intimately as often as he could. When they sailed off from the British coast, he was confident that his ship and all aboard were at the height of efficiency. Therefore, when their convoy came under enemy, aerial attack, the men saw it as trivial for a ship so well-prepared. They sustained little damage but could see one of their number at a distance completely afire.

Orders were given to move in, once the bombers had moved on, and the sight which greeted them was one of the most horrendous of the war. Bodies were hurling themselves off the vessel, into the sludge-grey of the sea, looking like so many rats leaving a sinking ship. From a distance, they could have been animals or small parcels, dropping down into the foam; the men did not care if they lived or died, only wanting to escape the kind of death dreaded by friend or foe, that of burning alive when the ship blew up.

Flames licked the funnels and deck-cabins and it was soon impossible to see an outline of the ship, as they moved in towards the patch of grey-green sea, which looked like a pond full of tadpoles. Rope ladders were flung over the sides and men from the cruiser let down rowing boats and life belts, in an attempt to save as many bodies as they could. As the sinking sailors were pulled up and literally shoved up the ladders, no thought was given for the safety of the men on board the healthy ship; all concentration was on rescuing their comrades from this scene of terrible destruction.

The officers watching the enflamed vessel knew that time was limited and before long the order was given to cease operations, long before all the drowning men were heaved out of the water. The cruiser departed, amidst screams and yells from those who were left and it was only just in time to avoid the colossal explosion and its after-effects. Andrew peered into the smoke, to see the remaining sailors sinking into turbulent water, knowing that those who were not killed by the sea were suffocated in heavy smoke. They had done their best and their ship was still afloat; that was the main thing.

Carrying many more personnel than they should, the Captain gave orders to return to a home port as quickly as possible, where the injured could be cared for. Little did Andrew know that this would be his last voyage because he had suffered massive lung damage whilst taking part in the rescue and the naval doctors declared him unfit for military service.

All through his wartime experiences, the only thing that Andrew had come to dread was to be disabled and hence laid off. Death to him was the only acceptable end to the war; anything less was futile and his diagnosis at Portsmouth Naval Hospital was one he could not accept.

"I tell you doctor, I am as fit as I've always been. You can't lay me up like a worn-out old fishing boat at the end of its working life. How old do you think I am, bloody sixty. I'm a young man and I've got a lot of fighting years left in me. All I've ever wanted to do is screw Hitler and his mob into the ocean like a bloody anchor. What do you think I can do on shore, write polite letters to the mothers of men who've snuffed it?"

"'Fraid so old chap. That's the way it is. Your poor old lungs won't last another month unless you take it easy. The smoke from that destroyer out there nearly did for you. You should be thankful…"

"Thankful? You expect me to be thankful because you're taking my life away! Oh yes, I'm bloody thankful alright, now I'm being put into dry dock. Well, I'll tell you one thing, Doc. You won't get any thanks from me!"

"Now, that'll do Petty Officer. Sort yourself out and get back to your ship to collect your things. I'm sure the Admiralty will find you something suitable. Good morning."

That was the end of it. Andrew wandered back down the maze of corridors, glowering at men in wheelchairs and men on crutches, never thinking that he was one of the lucky ones, only nursing his feelings of injustice and ferocious bitterness, until he reached the main door and walked off towards the quayside. He had been promoted to PO but a fat lot of good that would do him now.

CHAPTER 37

"I love you, I love you, Margaret," Henry said softly, into the fragrant strands of auburn hair, which curled down behind her ear.

"I love you too, Henry, but you really must stop this. My ear is all wet inside."

Why does she wear so much scarlet lipstick and dress herself up to the nines each day at college, if she doesn't want this kind of thing to happen, he wondered.

Her thin, pencilled eyebrows raised into perfect half-moons and she said gently, "I mean it, you know. I do love you a lot but I'm determined to finish my course and get a good job, if only to pay back my parents for being so good to me. You must understand. So, I think we have to make a pact not to let ourselves get too serious while we're studying, or I will have to keep away from you, just to be sure."

"You don't mean that, do you Margaret? That would be the worst thing that could happen to me, losing you because of my own stupid behaviour. You're right. We have to concentrate on university work until our courses are over. Then, we can start to think about our relationship again; that is if you don't meet somebody you like better."

"I doubt that very much. I said I loved you didn't I and I rarely change my mind. Come and give me a kiss and let's go downstairs. They kissed gently and lovingly and Margaret took out her handkerchief and wiped round the inside of her ear, while Ben, her dog, looked on from his prone position on the soft rag rug. She took out a powder compact from her handbag and deftly replaced the scarlet mouth which had been kissed off by Henry, then they left the sea-chest and opened the door to let the patient dog out. He immediately started barking and Henry rushed forward to grab him by the collar and chastise him.

"What on earth's the matter with you, boy? Don't make so much noise or we'll have mother charging up here to find our little hideaway."

Round the corner of the stairs came Jane, who appeared to be heading in their direction but as soon as she saw them she changed her mind and walked away at right-angles into her bedroom.

"Oh hello, you two," she said, looking round as she turned the corner. "I didn't expect to see you in the spare room. There's nothing there but rubbish. I keep my remnants of fabric in that chest of drawers and all the haberdashery left over from sewing jobs."

"We just went in to have a look at your old sea-chest, Jane. It's a very old one, isn't it?" said Margaret diplomatically.

"Yes dear. It was given to me by an old lady who used to live next door to us in Ecclesmachan. She said it belonged to her father, who went to sea with it and, sadly, it came back without him because he was killed in the last war."

"Oh, how miserable but what an interesting story. I'm surprised you don't keep it downstairs, in pride of place."

"No. It has always been hidden away for aesthetic reasons. You see, it's a rough old piece and has no place beside the varnished and polished furniture downstairs. I love it because it was given to me by a very dear friend but it couldn't be called a fine piece of furniture, not by any stretch of the imagination."

"I suppose you're right but surely it could be used for storage – of your winter clothes for example?"

Jane was tiring of this conversation and expected the girl to want to look inside the chest at any moment. Such a curious person was sure to find the hidden compartment and she had to avoid that opportunity at all costs.

"Why don't you both come down and I'll give you a piece of cake. I've just finished icing a chocolate one, your favourite Henry."

That did it and she ushered them in front of her down the rickety stairs. Her diary would have to wait, until she had perfect peace. Rob was not expected for another hour or so. When the house was quite empty, they still went up to the chest in the spare bedroom, just for old times, and sat there side by side, talking about events past and present as they had before. He had no idea that she still kept a regular journal and that they sat above her collection of lined, hard-backed books. Her writing was the one thing that kept her sane when they had serious discussions, or if there was a problem which she would rather not share with him. All she did was write it down and, as if by magic, the problem was solved. The invisible spirit of the exercise book disentangled any webs of dispute. After their tea and cake, Margaret decided to go home. They had already walked the dog along the burn and he was starting to fidget around and put his square head on one of their knees, as a hint that it was his tea-time also. Eventually it became too tedious to bear and they both walked slowly to the front door.

"I'll come with you if you like," said Henry, as he put his arm around Margaret's shoulders.

"No, it's quite alright, Henry. I must rush back and get on with some work for university. I left it 'til the last minute as usual and it has to be in by tomorrow. I'll see you at lunch-time tomorrow, if that's alright?"

"Of course it is. Just because we've had a serious conversation doesn't mean I don't care about you. I think what you said was very sensible and I intend to behave myself in future."

She started to put on her coat, they smiled then kissed and Margaret walked with Ben down through the still-overgrown garden.

Perhaps I'll have a go at finishing that mess this weekend, thought Henry. It would be something to take my mind off other things and I certainly need something to take my mind off them. As he stood on the doorstep, waving at the retreating figure of Margaret, who was constantly having to stop so that Ben could perform up a lamp-post or a garden fence, Rob's van drew up outside the cottage. He jumped out and slammed the door behind him, then retraced his footsteps and opened it again. When he reappeared, he was carrying a huge bunch of lilies, wrapped in newspaper.

"I almost forgot my peace-offering," he said, as he breezed past Henry and went inside.

Just like a husband, thought Henry.

CHAPTER 38

Andrew settled in to shore duty, although he had never thought he could take to it after such a thrilling time in the first half of the war. Certainly, 'Needs must when the devil drives' applied to him because he saw his near-infirmity as a devil he could live without but he now knew he was lucky in having any kind of role in the navy, after being certified unacceptable for normal duty.

Having so much time to think, which he found he could do while he shuffled papers and applied his signature to sheaves of munitions orders, his mind drifted on to the subject of Stephanie. What could he have been thinking of when he decided not to visit his mother during his shore leaves in Britain. He could have found out more about his girl from mum, couldn't he? She can't think much of him now. And no doubt she had the whole mess chasing after her, wherever she was posted. He must write to Henry again and find out what was going on in Scotland because his mother couldn't think much of him either. Finding out that his father had taken up with some posh hussy from Edinburgh had not surprised him in the slightest but hearing that the family house had been kept by him did. What sort of man let his wife and son move into a little cottage, while he lorded it over their big, stone mansion?

A rating came into the office with an order for materials for a submarine which was being refurbished at the docks, so he snapped alert and dealt with it, pushing his private thoughts to the back of his mind as work took over.

There was a friendly Wren called Frances, a Radar Operator in his building, who was constantly enquiring about him. She seemed so interested that he felt he could approach her with his request, which was more like an enquiry for advice than anything.

One morning, he spotted her in the corridor and rushed along the clinically bare passageway in order to catch up with her.

"Frances, I'm sorry to jump on you like this but I wondered if you could spare me a minute," he said, panting a little because of his breathing difficulties. He must try to remember not to dash around as he used to.

"Of course, Andrew. How can I help?"

She was so pleasant. Didn't even want to know what it was in advance, before saying yes.

"I wondered if you could advise me on what kind of perfume I could get for my ... er ...mother." He had to lie. What girl would want to help him to choose a scent for his girlfriend, not that Stephanie was.

"That would be lovely," she said and they arranged to meet in the canteen later that day.

It was obvious from the start that one lunch-time would not solve Andrew's problem and, after making a few notes on the back of old order forms, he decided to tear them up and invite Frances to his place to tell her a bit more about his mum, now she had moved out of their big house and into a cottage.

ooo

"We used to live in Ecclesmachan when I was a lad. That was before my parents split up." It was still embarrassing to tell anyone but it wouldn't get better by pretending it never happened.

"Did I hear you say, Ecclesmachan?"

"You did. That's where I used to live as a child."

"Then you must know where I lived. It's a place on the old Edinburgh to Glasgow canal called Ratho."

"I know it well. My father used to take my brother and I to Ratho when we were wee."

"I should have recognized the accent. You come from West Lothian, don't you? Even though you sound a bit posh."

"I do indeed and, now you come to mention it, I can hear the same burr in your voice. The posh bit is the private school I went to. And the trouble with being in the Navy is that you meet men from all over the British Isles and your accent gets changed by them as well. All it takes is to meet someone from home and it all comes rushing back, don't you think, hen?" He remembered all those times down at the burn with his Uphall pals.

"Aye, lad, I do."

They had a good laugh and then realised that lunch-time was over, so both went back to their own departments, nursing the thought that they would meet up later and go off to Andrew's digs. It was strange that his very reason for meeting up with Frances suddenly became extremely unnecessary. Stephanie might not come home very often, so his perfume could be sitting on a shelf for months. What had he been thinking about?

However, the evening went well and they sat and talked about places they had visited and people they knew. The road between Ratho and Ecclesmachan was described in detail and various short cuts and pathways through meadows filled with cows and horses were compared, each feeling theirs was the quicker and more beautiful. When Frances eventually went back to her rooms, a true friendship had been made, which was destined to support each one of them in times of trouble during that last difficult year of the war.

000

When hostilities ceased, they both knew where they would go first. Their destination was Ratho because they had talked about it so much. Andrew met all Frances's relatives and stayed with her cousin in his little farm cottage. Then one day they decided to go to Ecclesmachan to see the house where he had been brought up.

"I'm sure you'll think it a great big pile of stones, Frances. It's nothing like as cheerful as the house where your folks live. Nor do we have any cousins and aunts and uncles the way you do." He had to downplay the dreadfully large manor house, in case she thought him as big a snob as his father.

But Frances had made up her mind that Andrew was the man for her; he had all the contacts and, presumably the money, to help her on her climb up the social scale to better things. Although she found it difficult to relax when he went on about his brother at university and his father in the shale oil industry, this was the life she wanted. Had she made a big mistake, taking him to meet her family in Ratho? The idea was to find out whether he was a snob or just a nice guy with an uppercrust background.

"I'm sure I'll like it," she said, wondering whether he would inherit at some stage.

When the bus arrived in Uphall and they had talked about Andrew's future plans, Frances began to wonder if she had done the right thing in continuing their friendship after they were demobbed. Although she had lived in a small country village when she was young, the whole reason for her joining the navy was so that she could become something more than a country bumpkin. Her idea of the perfect life was to live in a city and frequent busy restaurants and shops. It seemed that Andrew wanted to go back to the soil.

After a long trudge, longer than any mile Frances had ever marched, they arrived outside a big stone-built house. Mansion was the name that flew into her mind. What was she doing here? It was right out in the country, nowhere near the big department stores and the city lights. But she could make sure she had a car and she was sure Andrew would change, once he was back in civvy street.

"Right, Frances, this is the place. I haven't been home all through the war and it comes as a bit of a shock to see the old barn again. I imagined it would be totally different somehow. And yet Henry wrote to me that dad still lives here, with a new wife of course."

"Oh, poor Andrew. You shouldn't have come, you know. I thought you said your mother lived in the same area. Why don't we go and see her?"

Before Andrew could answer yea or nay, the front door opened and out walked a decidedly sophisticated lady, wearing high heeled shoes and a lot of face make-up.

"What do you think you're doing here? Make yourself scarce and hurry up about it," she said, in a pseudo-posh voice.

Andrew didn't feel like speaking to this annoying person and turned to pull a face at Frances, who was standing behind him, goggle-eyed. At that point, the door opened again and he saw the back of his father, locking up the main door. Without waiting for him to turn around, the woman said,

"Michael, we have trespassers. I told you we should have a padlock on the front gate."

Then he turned around rapidly, an expression of fury on his once handsome face and saw Andrew and the girl.

"Andrew, what are you doing here?" he asked and then realised what he had said and tried to correct himself. "Well, obviously you have come to see your father but what I meant was, why didn't you let me know you were coming. I could have arranged to be in all afternoon. Instead of which, we are going out to visit friends in Edinburgh ..." His voice dwindled to a breath, as he waited for some reaction from Andrew.

There was a rather-too-long silence, then the son looked into the eyes of the father and said,

"It's alright, Dad. You don't need to be around. I just thought I'd show my friend where I used to live when I was under your ... thumb."

"You haven't learnt many manners in the navy, boy. I can see that much. But why don't you come back tomorrow and we can have a long talk."

"No thanks. I'll have a look round the policies and leave you to your socialising."

All this time, the woman stood with one hip raised and her arms folded over her ample bosom. Hanging from her hand, from the scarlet fingertips, was a snakeskin handbag and Frances took a delight in noticing that her high heeled shoes were navy blue; the bag matched nothing, so it must have been expensive and she wanted to show it off.

The older couple walked across to the Railton which was parked on the gravel in front of the house. Before they got in, Michael turned to speak to Andrew but, in his now accepted rude manner, Andrew took hold of Frances's arm and steered her round to the back of the house.

"At least he could have given you a key," she said, wondering why the two men were on such poor terms when Andrew had only just returned from the war.

"That would not be my father. He would be worried I would walk off with the silver." He took a long, hard breath, then let go of her arm. Frances was quite glad about this because he had been digging his fingers into her flesh and she was wondering when the pain would stop. "Come on, lass, I'll show you round the back."

There was nothing much to see, apart from a brand new building, which they saw was a double garage. Another car was still in there and Andrew saw it was a slightly smaller one than they had left in; it was a Ford.

"I thought you said you had a big garden at the back of the house. This garden looks no bigger than my parents'."

"He must have built on it, for his precious motorcars. My mother was the gardener."

Having said her name, Andrew desperately wanted to see her. But he was unsure whether he wanted Frances to accompany him. She was alright but not exactly the kind of girl mum would like. Oh, what was wrong with him? He was going out with Frances. His mother would have to accept his choice. His independent streak was appearing more and more.

000

So they did the long walk once more, in reverse order and, by the time they reached Jane's cottage, it was late afternoon. In the lane there were birds everywhere, flying in and out of the trees and calling constantly. This was more like it, a little piece of the real countryside. He knew where Rob had lived and there was only one other cottage beside his place. It was unnecessary to guess whether it was his mother's because there she was, a hoe in her hands and a pile of weeds at her feet. Andrew's heart started to beat wildly. He found it hard to believe that he had been away for so long, without a word to say he was safe, without a visit when he had his short leaves. How cruel could a man get?

As they approached the gate, Jane looked up to see who was coming along the old track. Her eyesight must be going because she squinted, with her hand up to her forehead.

"Hello, Mum," Andrew said, quietly. There was nothing wrong with her hearing because she flung down the hoe and almost tripped over her pile of vegetation, in her hurry to grab the gate latch.

"Oh Andrew, oh, my boy. How wonderful to see you so unexpectedly. What a lovely thing to do. You know I love surprises."

How different from his father.

Andrew left Frances's side and rushed to the now open gate. He clutched at his mother's outstretched arms and put his head down on her shoulder. The only word he said was,

"Mum," and that was all Jane wished to hear.

CHAPTER 39

They were ushered into the spotless little cottage and told to sit down, although Andrew just wanted to wander around and check out his mother's new space. He could already see some of her old possessions and much of the furniture from the big house. But how could she live in such a small area, having owned a mansion house in the not too distant past.

"You must have a cup of tea, both of you. I'm sure you had a bracing walk from the village."

Neither of them chose to tell her how much of a bracing walk had been taken, from Uphall to Ecclesmachan and back again, within the space of an hour. Frances felt she had to say something, as Andrew had gone mute. "That would be lovely," she said, in the way of an afternoon tea guest.

"I'll just put the kettle on and get some cake," Jane half-sang as she went through to the kitchen. Then she dashed back and said, "Oh, I'm so sorry, I completely forgot. Stephanie was putting on the kettle for the two of us, when you arrived. Let me run and get her. She'll be delighted to see you."

Andrew's face had gone pale. He stood up. He looked first at Frances and then at his mother's receding back.

"Stephanie's here?" he said. She must have been demobbed at the same time as them.

"That's what she said. Who's Stephanie anyway?" Frances asked pettishly.

Andrew was, for the first time in ages, non-plussed. Why was Stephanie at his mother's house? This was an embarrassing situation. Worse than that, it was an impossible situation. How could he face her?"

The kitchen door opened and his mother appeared, followed by a girl he hardly recognized. So this is what Stephanie had become? A lovely woman tagged along behind his mum. No, no-one could say Stephanie tagged in their wildest dreams. This Stephanie held her head high and her back straight, straighter than most ratings he had seen recently. Her hair was held back with an alice band and her brown eyes shone in a face which was tanned by the country sunshine. She wore masculine gardening clothes, which only served to make her look more feminine. And she was wearing thick socks. Stephanie.

"Hello Andrew," she said in a much lower register than any woman had the right to possess.

"Hello Stephanie," he replied and they stood, looking at each other.

"I'm Frances," Frances broke in, with her girlish voice, and the spell was broken.

"Oh, of course, I'm being very rude," Jane said. "This is Andrew's friend from the navy, Frances. My dear, you must meet Stephanie. We've known her since she was a little girl, you know. And she was in the navy as well, so you'll have lots to talk about."

Thank goodness for a mother. Even though Stephanie had hardly been a little girl at Boys' Brigade camp, it served to make her sound like an old family friend.

The rest of tea-time was taken up with anecdotes of a casual nature from Andrew and it was very obvious that he did not want to discuss the war and the part he had played in it. He was loathe to upset his mother, now the war was over, so he kept his comments light and avoided any talk about the way the Service operated. As part of the conversation, Stephanie dropped a bombshell. Henry had said she had joined up in one of his letters but didn't say much more. So when she told Andrew that she had been working as a radar operator for the navy at Rosyth it was definitely a surprise. He had imaged her in the Land Army or somesuch. But, after her mention of the navy, Frances started to make comments about her own work and expected Stephanie to join in with anecdotes of her own, regarding the officers and men, and the subordination of women in the ranks. Much to her disgust, Stephanie would not play her game and Andrew wanted to stop Frances from continuing. After all, Frances was his girl now and there was no need for her to be jealous of Stephanie.

CHAPTER 40

Both Henry and Margaret received their exam results on the same day. Margaret was delighted and gushed all over Henry when they met for lunch. She waved her hands in the air and put her arms around him in public, not seeming to notice that everyone else in the dinner queue was watching.

"Here! Hold on would you! You're covering me in your foul, red lipstick!" he said, after she had finished.

Not knowing how to handle this complete change in manner, Margaret immediately calmed down and looked down pensively at the floor. What was she doing that was so bad? Her results had shown her that she could do well in her finals and that was all she ever wanted in life. It was alright for Henry, he always did well, although you would never think so.

"I'm sorry, Henry. I just got carried away when I realised that there really is a chance that I will become a doctor. You know how desperately I want to pay back my parents for all their kindness. They've lived in niggardly circumstances as long as I can remember, so that we children could do well and there seems to be a chance…"

"Would you just shut up for a minute, Margaret. You're driving me mad. Nobody else is behaving like this because of a few examination results."

"Alright. If that's the way you want it, I'll sit somewhere else. I suppose it would be asking too much to hear how you did?"

"I got 80% in most subjects and a 75."

"But that's wonderful. Now you can relax for a while."

"Oh, you think that do you? I think it's bloody awful. Anybody could do that. I'd set my heart on reaching the 90s this time, due to all the extra work I've put in but what do I get, a ridiculous 80 – and a 75 what's more! It must be due to all the weekends I've spent in Uphall. Well, that can stop now. I intend to get better marks in my degree exams."

"Now, come on, Henry…"

"Don't 'come on Henry' me. I know what I want and I'm going to get it. If I don't, there are always plenty of tall buildings in Edinburgh. Now, leave me alone, Margaret. I want to think things out."

She took her tray of food to the other side of the refectory and ate it in silence. Every now and again, she looked up to see what Henry was doing and all she could see was the top of his head, as he scribbled in his little black book and a hand shot out from time to time to grab his cup of coffee. This was totally unexpected.

However, Henry meant what he had said and there were no more cosy weekends at his mother's house, no more rambles in the countryside. If he had only known, Margaret had more offers of male company than she could handle and even stopped going to the refectory for lunch to avoid the myriad offers. There were some occasions when she felt extremely tempted to accept an evening at the cinema, just to prove she was still attractive. Henry was not the only fish in the pond.

000

Several weeks later, as he rounded the corner of the corridor and prepared to descend stone steps at the side of the building, he stopped. He could smell Margaret's perfume. It was light and lemony and he knew it so well, that he stood and looked around, knowing she was around. So he kept marching on, down the wide passageway and turned a sharp corner, heading towards a lecture room.

She was standing behind a wall, in the short corridor leading to the Ladies and Gents, wiping her nose on a piece of Bronco, the hardest toilet paper in the world. He had felt indefinite about their erstwhile relationship but seeing her sobbing there, alone, he realised how much rapport had been between them.

He tipped up her chin and stared into her lovely, weepy eyes, loving the sight of them, even like this. She just stood there and let him gather her into his arms, enjoying the roughness of his sweater on her wet face and the musky smell of him as he bent her head down onto his firm chest. It felt as if no time at all had passed since their walks with Ben, their cuddles on the sea chest and their lingering goodnight kisses. How had she lived without him? His voice was decidedly muffled by her woolly cardigan, but he managed to say,

"Margaret, I'm sorry. I didn't mean to hurt you. I was just so horrified at my results, after all my hard work. But I realise now that you mean more to me than any exam results in the world."

"Do you mean that, Henry?" she asked in a nasal, tearful, croaky voice.

"Of course I do. I'm actually relieved that it's all out in the open, so much so that I want you to come to mother's with me at the weekend. I'm going to be a different person from now on – and to hell with my results. I suppose I'm doing as well as most of the chaps I know."

Margaret knew Henry always did what he promised, so she looked forward to a trip to see his mother.

CHAPTER 41

The weekend arrived and two heads passed the cottage window on the way to the front door. Jane had been sitting on the sofa in the window and moved out of sight when she saw them arrive. She wanted to jump up and fling open the door but forced herself to play the authoritarian mother for a while, to make Henry suffer a tiny bit for all the heartache he'd put her through these past few weeks. At least it made her feel in charge as she let them knock a few times.

When Jane eventually brought them into the room, she hugged Margaret first, then Henry. It was good to see her son again and she liked Margaret very much; she could see that he did also.

They both walked into the living room and sat down together on the sofa. Nothing was said and Jane felt she must break this dreadful silence.

"Henry, I know you've had your exam results. I suppose you have as well, Margaret. Was it good news for both of you?" Why hadn't he contacted her?

Margaret looked at Henry, wondering if he would denigrate his results to his own mother and Henry looked at Margaret, hoping she would keep quiet about his ranting and raving. He need not have worried because she was the first one to speak.

"I'm happy to tell you, Mrs Donaldson, that my results were all I hoped for. I'll let Henry tell you about his, of course."

Henry felt that was an extremely diplomatic answer, but then she would need all her social skills when she became a doctor. They were renowned for their bedside manner.

"Yes, Mum, I did well too," he smiled, at Margaret, then at his mother. "Of course I worried terribly when I did the exams and then again when I knew the results were coming out – but that's me, isn't it. You must have known why I avoided coming to see you; I was terrified and had to keep to myself until I knew."

Would he ever change. Jane wondered if this sensible girl would be the making of him. If anybody could keep him calm, it would be Margaret. "I'm very pleased for both of you. And now I expect you would like the celebratory chocolate cake; is that right my boy?"

"Of course it is."

What would life be without Mum's chocolate cakes at each anniversary, each exam result and each homecoming. He had heard that Andrew had returned to the fold. He hoped he was treated to a chocolate cake as well. Henry had spoken to Andrew and knew a little of his visit with his girl Frances. Seemingly Stephanie had been there as well, which couldn't have made for a relaxing visit. He thought that Stephanie had been The One but now he had Frances, so maybe things had changed.

Jane went out to the kitchen to put some tea things on a tray and Henry shuffled closer to Margaret.

"I know this isn't the way it should be, Margaret, but I can't put the idea out of my head. Margaret, I wonder if you would consider doing me the honour of becoming my wife?"

It came as such a surprise that Margaret started to laugh.

"Oh, if that's the way you feel, I wish I hadn't bothered. I had the feeling that you liked me and that we got on very well together. Forget it."

This was dreadful. How could she put right her foolish behaviour? At that moment, Jane reappeared bearing a full tray, with the proverbial chocolate cake and some home-made biscuits. She felt Henry stiffen beside her and knew it had to be now or never, so she said,

"Thank you Henry. I laughed at you just now but I didn't mean to trivialize your question. It just came as such a surprise."

"What question was that, dear," Jane said, conversationally.

"Henry asked me to marry him and I burst out laughing."

"Oh," was all she could say. Had she turned him down and was that why her son was sitting like an automaton, his body erect and his knees together?

"Well, you know what it's like when someone poses an important question, just when you had started thinking about your afternoon tea?"

Jane said, "Yes," still with no expression on her face and a full tray in her hands.

"I began to laugh, from nervousness, nothing else."

The two faces in front of her were identical, in lack of expression and with questioning brows.

"Now I've accepted the seriousness of the question, I want to answer but it feels strange giving you an answer, Henry, with your mother in the room."

"Please don't worry about me, Margaret. I've left the teapot in the kitchen and I must collect it and the strainer and the sugar bowl," and she quickly put down the heavy tray on the table in the centre of the room and dashed back the way she had come.

Not wanting to make him suffer any longer than he needed to, Margaret took hold of Henry's cold hand and looked into his serious face, saying,

"Yes, Henry. I accept your wonderful offer. I have longed to hear you say those words."

"Really," he almost shouted. "You mean you'll have me?"

"I certainly will," she said but omitted to say that she wanted to finish her degree course before even thinking about getting married. No doubt he did as well. But he just carried on being excited and said,

"Then let's call mother. We have a great need for her chocolate cake now!"

Jane was hovering in the doorway and had no need to be called. She had been terrified that Margaret would turn him down, because he was such a sensitive boy and hated disappointments. It was such a lovely feeling for her to know that he had put all his fears behind him and decided to enter into a true relationship at last. She felt like jumping up and down in the excitement of the moment but those were only her inner feelings and she knew she must behave like the older woman she was. Smiles and kisses were what the engaged couple received.

She longed to tell Rob.

CHAPTER 42

So long ago, Jane had agreed with Rob that their lives were good the way they were. She had shown no need for further formality in the form of a wedding band and a shared house; in fact it had never been mentioned.

He knew, however, he was being selfish in every respect. Jane was the perfect woman. She cooked for him, mended his clothes, took his boots to the cobbler, in fact she did everything a wife would do, without expecting the respect that marriage would bring from other people. How could he know what gossip she endured by being what they thought was a 'bidey-in' but she was not in fact even that. And that was something he longed for, in the dead of the night when he was totally alone, even though he had been the one who had mentioned non-commitment first.

000

Next day, Rob walked to the back door of the cottage he knew so well – in fact the gardens had been laid out like one big plot and there was no fence between the two houses at the back. He knocked. He should knock. There had been far too many occasions when he had simply walked into the kitchen and called. Respect was an essential word in every relationship and he had shown Jane none, feeling that affection did away with the esteem he had felt for her, all through the years.

"Who's there?" He heard her voice call, from the living room.

"It's me - Rob!" he shouted.

"Then why don't you come in? Are you carrying something heavy. Let me help you."

"No, dear, I'm not carrying anything, apart that is from a hefty guilty feeling."

"What on earth are you talking about, Rob?" she said, appearing at the back door.

"I want to talk to you, Jane."

"Come on in and let me make you a bite to eat."

"No! Not until I've spoken to you. I've had something on my mind for quite a while."

"Well, you know you can talk to me. Let's have a comfortable seat?"

They sat down together on the soft, brown velvet and Rob put his hands between his knees, before raising them up in a praying attitude to his mouth.

"I want to talk seriously, about us. Seeing Henry and his girl pass my window and Andrew and his naval friend the other day made me realise that we can't go on like this, Jane. So, I want you to marry me. Be my wife in name as well as in deed, because that's what you are."

"What a surprise! I never expected you to ask me."

"Why not?"

"Because, you're not the marrying kind, that's why."

"Let me be the judge of that, if you please. I have been nursing my resentment for my father for too long. Now you have shown me how happy we can be together and I want you to marry me. Please say you will."

Proposals must come in twos like the local buses. There was a silence that seemed to travel around the room, searching for a place to hide. Jane's and Rob's faces were set in thoughtful expressions, until a blackbird in the tree outside the window broke the spell by beginning to trill out its happiness. Rob took hold of her hand and raised it gently to his mouth, kissing each tight knuckle in an attempt to relax Jane's tenseness. She turned to face him, looking into his dark green, sensitive eyes, which had lost their brooding expression and sat soulfully staring out at her.

"I'm sorry, Rob. I can't."

Even Jane was surprised by her reaction. She had longed for this moment, since the first time she had seen Rob in the garden next door but, over the years, she had come to accept their unusual relationship as the only one which could work for them. Alright, every so often she wanted to be a respectable married woman again. However, if she accepted Rob's kind request, which was done to please her and take away the stigma of a lone woman half-living with a man, she would lose him forever.

She knew that, without further discussion. In fact she sensed it, from the depths of her subconscious mind.

"I can't because I know you too well. Don't get me wrong. I don't mean I know you and don't want you. I mean I understand the workings of your complicated mind and you are a wild thing, not to be tamed. Let's enjoy our lives the way they are. I'm happy, if you are."

Having worked up the courage to propose, Rob's pride hurt intensely, now that he had been refused. He would have to get out of this house. He had to get into the garden, as quickly as possible. So, with several sentences of excuse, he raised his lithe body into an upright position, stretched and smiled falsely, then left. Jane wandered through her cottage, straightening cushions and curtains, flattening bedspreads, picking up pieces of fluff from the stair runner, until she had used up her emotional energy and felt able to sit down again. She knew she had done the right thing. It might take Rob a little longer but she knew he would agree with her decision, eventually.

000

In Uphall, Stephanie was suffering the same fate as Rob, only not regarding the same subject. When she had arrived home, after the tea party, she remembered how quiet and introspective Andrew had been when they met, the way she had felt the whole time he had been away in the war. But eventually they had started to talk, including Frances and Jane of course.

He said he intended to open a carpenter's workshop in the sleepy little village of Ratho and the purchase documents had already been signed. That was where Frances and her family lived and she had agreed to run the front shop – which was in fact part of a renovated barn next to the cottage where he would live. His life was almost organised. And yet he still sounded uncertain. Stephanie knew him so well and understood the nuances in his voice. Was he going to marry that girl? She seemed too wild and brazen for him.

000

Andrew had left his mother's cottage in total confusion. Why had Stephanie been there? Before seeing her, he had intended to settle down with Frances. After all, they had swapped stories of their respective families and it had seemed like the right thing to do. Now he had made an offer for the workshop and cottage out at Ratho with marriage in mind. His arrival at his mother's place that day had almost persuaded him that there was no time like the present. As he walked through her door, he had almost proposed to Frances. Then, Stephanie had appeared.

When he had looked into mum's kitchen, it had been so good to see her array of cooking implements, which were arranged as they had been in the much larger kitchen of his youth. Big bunches of sage and thyme hung down from the ceiling and he was tall enough to rub his head beneath them and smell their earthy fragrance. Then, Stephanie.

He had never asked Frances if she would continue to work, now she was home; he had just accepted that she would want to help him in his new business. Women were returning to normal lives now; looking after their menfolk; bringing up children. In his mind, the old-fashioned back door had clicked open and his wife stood there, laden down with shopping bags all in one hand, as she lifted the catch – but he realised now that it had been Stephanie in his dreams, not Frances.

CHAPTER 43

It must have taken two weeks for Andrew to change his life. He spoke to Frances, who seemed to have been expecting that particular conversation.

"I knew when you spoke to that girl in your mother's cottage that she was your old flame. The sparks were flying, even as we all chatted together. Andrew, you put the fire out in *my* heart, the minute you said 'Hello Stephanie'. But I'm not terribly upset. I hope you don't mind, but I feel we were never meant to go the full voyage together. You're too countrified and I want to be a sophisticated townie. Let's call it a day. Our particular watch is over."

He was so grateful to her, even with her mixed metaphors. What other woman would have taken such a disappointment on the chin, the way Frances did. But here he was, still thinking of her as one of the crew, one of the lads. His big ideas of moving to Ratho and starting a business as a carpenter were a bit out of this world. Anyway, they probably needed carpenters in Uphall.

So, he had cancelled his offer to buy the workshop and Frances had said she would take the cottage to be near her family and it was all done.

When he went to see Jane the next time, he was hoping Stephanie would be there again, but no such luck.

000

Andrew knew exactly what he would do next. His longing to see Stephanie was all-encompassing. Life without her, now that they had re-met, was something he could not envisage and the sooner he discovered how she felt about him, the better. He knew where she lived.

As he walked down the little street on the edge of Broxburn, he remembered the only other time he had called at her house. On that occasion she had sent him off with no word of comfort, saying she was far too young to have a regular boyfriend. Now she had lived away from home and done a responsible job in the navy and he was quite amazed that she had returned to her family home, where her mother was a drunken mess and her father had forbidden the company of boys for so long.

The collection of cottages had been built for shale oil workers and were called the 'rows'. The fronts of the buildings looked to all extents and purposes like the back doors of other houses, with washing hanging limply on lines and drainpipes down the walls. These were poor dwellings and yet he had accepted them as a part of life when he lived in the area. The oil industry had a lot to answer for. They flung up tiny houses for their workers, wherever there was an acre of space and they were so well flung up that they would probably last forever. Eyesore was the word that sprang to mind. The oil industry had begun to decline here after the First World War, so men had returned to the coal mining they left for better conditions, or they went back to farming. Perhaps the rural way of life would be re-established in the place of dirt and grime.

This was her door, he was certain. He remembered the blue paint, which was so different from that of their neighbours, who stuck to the dull green of an industrial time. It must have been Stephanie's influence that instigated such brightness. She had always been one for difference.

He rang the bell. He stood at attention, his arms by his sides and waited. There were footsteps coming down the uncarpeted hall, which were much more frightening than enemy gunfire. What would he say to her? How would she reply to him? In seconds he would know. The door handle turned and it was pulled towards someone, but only slightly, so that a pair of eyes could peer through the crack. He could see blonde peroxided hair and a mouth still wearing last night's lipstick colour. This must be the mother. The mother who worked in a bar in the evening, then slept most of the next morning away. He glanced down at his wrist- watch and noticed that it was mid-day.

"Hello, is Steph ... I mean, could I speak to Stephanie, please."

He felt like a small boy, asking if his friend could come out to play. What was he thinking about? He was a grown man. He drew himself up even further and placed his hand on the side of the door, pushing it slightly forward, so the half-hidden woman would have to speak to him, if only to ask him to desist.

But she smiled, which surprised him, and said,

"Of course, hen. I'll give her a shout" and she crowed into the room behind her, "Steph, there's a young man at the door and he's asking for you."

Andrew could hardly bear the suspense. He wondered if Stephanie would also look like this crone, when she wasn't expecting visitors. He wondered whether she would send him packing as she had all those years ago. But he need not have worried.

She came to the door and quietly told her mother to go and get dressed. Without an ounce of embarrassment, she called back,

"I won't be long, mother. I'm just going for a short walk."

She grabbed a coat from a chair inside the door, then closed it behind her, feeling in her pocket for her keys, as she did.

"Let's walk along the canal," she said, in a perfectly normal, calm voice, as if she had been doing this for years.

Andrew could hardly get the word out to say, "Okay" and they walked off down the little street, between the skipping games which had just started and the calling of the young boys, singing, 'We know where you're going'.

On reaching the narrow path beside the weedy water, Stephanie turned to Andrew and said,

"Was it something important, that brought you down to the boon-docks this morning – or is it afternoon now?"

He had been rehearsing for hours, so it took no time at all for Andrew to say, in his straightforward way; no messing about, no bended knee; nor even a pointed look in her direction. There was no need. They were the only ones on the path. "Yes, it was very important," he said. "I want you to marry me. Will you, Steph?"

She took hold of his hand and looked into his worried eyes and said, equally calmly,

"Yes. It's only taken me five and a half years to decide, so it might be the wrong decision." Her words were slightly humorous but totally serious.

Pulling her towards him excitedly, Andrew enveloped her in a huge bear-hug, which lasted several minutes until they eventually parted. And looking into each others' eyes, they kissed.

000

They married by special licence, as if the war were still on, after Andrew had secured a lovely little cottage near one of the outlying farms at the end of the village. Only his mother and Rob attended apart from Henry and Margaret, who were their witnesses and they all stayed for a superb tea, made by Jane. It was as if the two had never been apart. The dreadful years of war melted away, to reveal a happily married couple in the land of their birth, surrounded by family.

All Stephanie wanted now was her own little family.

CHAPTER 44

Sadly, Stephanie did not become pregnant. Oh how sad she became, as the months rolled by and she thought she would never conceive.

Then there was a change and she knew it was happening. She desperately wanted someone to talk to, about this wonderful, new development in her life. It was so exciting and yet so worrying. A little conversation with someone her own age would sort out the colly-wobbles.

She little knew this was something Margaret had been hoping for, when Stephanie invited her to come to her house in the country for a cup of tea one afternoon in October. As she made her way to the farm cottage in the small country village, Margaret enjoyed the smells and sounds all around her. There was a field occupied by hairy Clydesdales, some adults and some youngsters still in their muted, reddish coats and they lifted their heads from the meager autumnal grass as she passed and lumbered to the gate.. They probably expected her to be the farmer arriving with their oats but happily stayed for a stroke on their soft, warm noses, regardless. In the distance, she could hear some barking noises and a huge mound of smelly manure over the fence reminded her that she was in the heart of farming country.

What a pleasant place in which to live. She was so glad that Stephanie and Andrew had settled fairly close to Jane because it meant they could visit each other easily. She had often wondered why they had no children of their own but it was just as well because they ran their little business together. Andrew was a fine carpenter and had obviously worked hard at his craft, after finding a local man to give him informal lessons; not exactly an apprenticeship but obviously very similar, as he had told them about following his mentor around from stately home to farmhouse, from Royal palace to bothy yard.

Their cottage was one long building which had been two smaller homes joined into one. To the right of this, there was a barn with huge slatted doors. This was the place then.

At her first timid knock, the partially glazed door opened instantly and Margaret knew she had been expected for some time.

"Hello Stephanie, I'm sorry I'm late," she said, as her coat was being pulled from her back unceremoniously.

They went into the front parlour and she was amazed at the modern interior, compared with the old-fashioned outside. There was chromium and pewter instead of the usual brass fittings of cottages of this genre and the room was completely carpeted, right up to the skirting boards, Navy Blue of course. A mirror without a frame perched above the mantelpiece, held together with some kind of clips on the wall. The only items recognisable as ornamentation were ships and boats, in china, pottery, in bottles and on the wall as pictures.

"I can see you find our décor a little unusual. We both decided to celebrate our times in the navy," said Andrew's wife. And Margaret had to say,

"Yes. It's so different, so unusual."

"Do you think so, Margaret? I hope we're not too unusual. You see, I wanted to tell you something, which will put us in the category of extremely ordinary married people."

They sat down on the pale grey linen settee and Stephanie continued,

"After a few months here, I had not conceived a child. What do the older people call it, 'fallen' for a baby, so I went to the quack and had some examinations and tests. Sorry, I know you are a doctor yourself, so I shouldn't say 'quack'. But he told me it was unlikely that I ever would have our own baby and Andrew was marvellous."

So that was the reason. Stephanie wanted her medical advice. But Stephanie's voice was excited and slightly highly pitched for her. There was no misery lurking in the short, sharp sentences, as she told Margaret about her inability to conceive. In fact, it was more like the opposite situation. And the young doctor was about to find out that what she had surmised was absolutely true.

"But I know now that the doctor was wrong and I'm expecting. I had guessed it for some months and didn't dare go to see the doctor again, thinking that I must be run-down or somesuch. But now I've been and he said I am probably about four months pregnant. What do you think of that?"

"It's wonderful, Stephanie. It really is. So what did you want to ask me? I presume that's why I'm here."

"Oh no, Margaret, not at all. I just needed to share my news with another woman. But I suppose I do want to ask your advice about one thing. You see I told Andrew that I was unable to have children and he was so good about it, that I haven't the heart to tell him I'm expecting ... in case ... in case it all goes wrong and we're disappointed again. Do you think I would be behaving selfishly if I kept it to myself for a bit longer ... just to make sure""

Margaret had heard many reasons for a wife not telling her husband she was going to have a baby but never such an unselfish one. Poor Stephanie, she must love Andrew very much to keep her secret from him, just so he didn't have to be disappointed if she aborted.

"Stephanie, I quite understand why you are doing this, but I'm sure Andrew can handle the situation, even if thing go wrong, which I don't think they will now, after four months. However," she said, putting on her family doctor's voice, "keep it to your self until you are five months pregnant and then tell him. Usually, any problems will have settled by that time. And you'll be starting to show, so you will have to tell him, won't you?"

Stephanie had been sitting on the edge of her seat, ingesting every word that Margaret said and she now replied,

"Oh thank you, my dear friend. I knew you would have some down-to-earth advice for me. I will hug my secret close to my chest for another few weeks."

Margaret was delighted. Stephanie had called her a dear friend. She would monitor the health of Andrew's wife herself and lead her into a healthy childbirth, come what may.

"I knew I did the right thing by inviting you over," Stephanie said.

"I am certainly enjoying myself, even though I worried before coming that you had some unsolvable problem. But then I'm used to that in my work. And now we can look forward to another little Andrew or Stephanie in a few months' time"

When she saw Henry again, Margaret omitted to tell him the reason for seeing Stephanie but she could tell he was happy that the two of them had become friends.

"What do you think about good old Rob hanging around such a lot? He really imagines he belongs at mother's," he said, changing the subject.

"I don't think you should worry about him. Your mother is in complete control of the situation and I expect they'll get married one of these days."

"I don't know if I want them to."

"I'm sorry, Henry, but I don't think it has anything to do with you."

"I suppose not but Andrew was the one who brought up the subject. He used to like Rob immensely when he was around such a lot in our childhood but now he seems to think he's playing games with mother. You would think he would have asked her to marry him by now."

"Oh stop it! They're much too mature to feel they have to answer to either of you. You're behaving as if they're the children and you're the older generation."

"And you're behaving like the family doctor. I know now what you must be like in the surgery."

"You have no idea, nor do I know what you're like in your laboratory, so why not lay down your weapons and let's have some supper."

CHAPTER 45

When Stephanie did tell Andrew that she was pregnant, it was as if she had given him an officer's commission. He strutted around for days, knowing they would be parents in a few months' time.

Telling the rest of the family was wonderful and Jane, particularly, loved the idea of being a grandmother. Margaret stayed true to her word and kept a close eye on Stephanie's behaviour, encouraging her to take plenty of exercise and the same amount of nourishing food as usual. The idea of 'eating for two' was not something she believed in and her surgery was full of trim young mothers, who eventually gave birth to equally healthy babies.

When it came to Stephanie's time to go into labour, she was taken to the local hospital, rather than giving birth at home, which had always been the norm in the past. And the modern ways certainly seemed to work.

The child was born in December and, by the time spring came, she, Fiona, was ready to come out of hiding in her shawls and blankets, to meet the warmest year they had known in Scotland, for centuries.

Jane was glad they lived so close because it meant she could collect the little one in her pram and walk up and down the main street of Uphall village, feeling like the Queen. In fact she felt like a queen most days now. Stephanie and Andrew were married with a little girl and Henry and Margaret were also married. There were no children expected for them yet but she knew that Margaret wanted to make a go of her career first and that Henry didn't mind in the slightest. Or at least that's what he said, if ever the subject came up.

000

Although Fiona could walk, she still needed a pushchair on long expeditions. The day which was to change all their lives forever started bright and still. A few clouds could be seen in the sky, as Andrew checked from the window, but they were of the stratus variety, which formed organza strips of white in the cobalt blue and melted lazily onto the mountain tops in the distance. The sun was unforgettably strong for a spring day and Stephanie and Andrew unbuttoned their coats, as they left the stone cottage, with Fiona in her pushchair, hearing the black metal gate swing squeakily on its hinges. Must bring some oil out for that, thought Andrew.

They had planned a trip to Linlithgow

The idea was to travel by bus to see the palace and feed the swans on the loch. Fiona's little pockets were full of crumbs, made painstakingly for her by Granny and squeezed down into the small, silky panniers of her best coat.

"I wish you would let me put your crumbs in a paper bag in my handbag for you, Fiona," Stephanie said, as she leant down once more to ensure the pocket flap was lying flat on top of the crummy treasure. The child clutched her coat pocket and looked beseechingly at her father, proving that children understand a lot more about possession than we think.

"It's just that it's such a long way and quite a time before we get there."

She pulled a face and only clutched harder.

Nothing more could be said. If Fiona decided on something, even at her age, that is exactly what she did. Trying to change her mind took much persuasion and had to be backed up with logical reasoning. Otherwise she was immovable. This child had been born an adult in disguise.

They arrived in Linlithgow and made their way past St Michael's Church, and down to the flat expanse beside the Palace wall.

"Did you know that Mary, Queen of Scots, was baptized in that big church, Stephanie?" said Andrew, trying to sound educational.

"Of course I did. I was born in this county, just like you."

"Alright, have it your own way. Let's go and find some birds to feed, my darling."

Stephanie was pleased to hear this endearment. Although it was time, Andrew had never called her by any affectionate name, as far as she could remember. Even though he held her and kissed her, he was not able to express his feelings in words.

Could it be that his father's example had rubbed off a little, even though it was the wrong kind?

They went to the grassy edge of the huge loch and before long several stately white swans sailed into view. They stayed a couple of yards away from the edge, swimming from side to side in unison, until Fiona flung her first handful into the water. Two swans reached out their long necks and retrieved the pieces of bread, lifting up their heads to swallow and then they waited patiently until the others had taken their share and came forward once again. The small child threw and giggled and eventually turned her pockets inside out into the water, until all her treasure had gone.

"They mate for life, you know," Andrew said, grinning at Stephanie.

"That sounds sensible," she replied. What happens if one dies, do they take another mate then.

"I don't really know; I think so. But all I remember is that an old man told me how they keep the same mate year after year and he showed me a single swan on the loch up the farm track who'd lost it's mate and was bringing up its young ones alone It made me feel quite miserable at the time."

"Well, my dear swan, you don't have to worry about that, do you", she said and he clutched her round the waist. This was more than she had expected.

They spent a little longer walking round the fine, sandstone walls and gazing up at the windows and gun slots, until the sun started to disappear behind the now racing clouds and Andrew felt it was time to leave.

As they waited for the bus which would take them home, a west wind started to blow around their feet and before long they had to hide in a shop doorway, pointing the pushchair inwards to avoid the swirls of dust which were collecting up and down the street. As the front of the bus came into sight, clouds were gathering in filthy profusion across the sky and there were spots of rain in the cold blasts of wind dashing down the wide main street of the historic town like a black, medieval knight on his charger.

"I didn't expect this today," said Stephanie.

"It was in the shipping forecast on the radio," said Andrew, putting his hand down to tuck in Fiona's hair.

"Do you still listen to that? Why?"

"Habit, I suppose. Quite often you can tell what kind of weather is coming by the direction and strength of the wind."

"You mean you can. Having spent all my naval time in an office, it doesn't apply to me."

"Anyway, I knew it was going to be windy but not that there would be a veritable gale before we got back home. I hope my mother has a good fire going when we get to Uphall. I just feel like a cup of tea by the hearth."

They got on and the bus chuntered along past fields of cows and horses and it was obvious from trees dividing green pastures that this was not merely a normally windy day. Some of the taller ones were bowing down and frightening the farm horses who were sheltering underneath them. Every so often a Clydesdale or a riding horse would gallop away from the field side, to stand staring from the middle ground at its braver friends.

Soon, they were climbing the hill between swooshing branches, travelling rockily round bends at the top where there was no protection at all and then the vehicle descended speedily to Uphall village at the bottom of the road. The day which had started off bright and calm had deteriorated into a noisy, squally wind-storm. The street lights were flickering on and off and some shops had completely dark interiors, as if fuses had blown in the gale.

"I do hope Jane's alright," Stephanie said, turning round to the other two. "This is more like a hurricane than the normal wind we've become used to."

"I think it would take more than a puff of wind to worry my mother, don't you?"

"I suppose you're right. I don't know why I'm being so silly about her. I'm sure she's been through worse than his in her long life."

They made their way along the main street and turned off to cross the bridge over the burn. Water swirled and splashed its way down the narrow gap between its steep banks and Andrew knew that later on there would be water coming through the planks to wet people's feet – if they were crazy enough to walk across it.

Jane's gate squeaked in its usual fashion and, pushing it closed again once they were on the garden path, was difficult even for Andrew. He made a joke for Fiona's sake about needing to eat more spinach like Popeye The Sailor Man in the comics, then they stood under the eves and Stephanie knocked at the door. They looked like a group of vagabonds begging for shelter, as they waited for Jane to let them in to the warmth of her comfortable old cottage.

CHAPTER 46

After lunch, Jane had cleared the dishes away then sat at the kitchen table in peace and quiet.

She knew what she would do. Bake a cake for the wanderers' return. They were coming back for tea. Her recipe books were on a shelf above her head and she twisted as she stood up and reached for Constance Spry. An old English friend had given this book to her, many years ago but the recipes were just as good now as they ever were. Jane enjoyed the descriptive prose which went with the list of ingredients, which didn't lay down definite rules but left it to the baker or meal-maker to decide how she would do it. That gave every woman in the kitchen the right to make up her own mind about her creations. It was the right time to make something more complicated than usual, as long as she had all the ingredients. She flipped the pages of the heavy, pink tome, until she decided on an apple upside-down cake. That would use up some of the apples she had stored in newspaper in the larder.

She took out her large mixing bowl and wiped the white inside with a dishcloth, noting that some of the yellow-ochre textured pottery on the outside had started to chip. It was hardly surprising when she remembered how long she had had it and how many Christmas cakes had been stirred in it. When the ingredients had been gathered together in their various packets, a vision of Andrew and Stephanie with Fiona, walking along the street in Linlithgow assailed her thoughts. Rob was next door and she knew now that he would remain there. Her life had become settled and it was time to behave like an older woman, who took delight in her grandchild, her garden and her needlework. Her family was close by and it was really time to settle down and be happy.

She stopped thinking and looked up at the window. It had become very dark and the clouds were lowering down onto the horizon in a heavy band of grey. She could hardly see to continue, so moved her chair back from the overloaded table with a loud scrape and went to light the paraffin lamp in the centre. She knew the young folk found her too old-fashioned, clinging to the old lamps which had been there since the houses had been built. It was about time she started to move with the times and put on the electric light, which had been installed a few weeks ago. That was a howling gale, baying at the substantial cottage door and rattling it on its heavy brass hinges. There was certainly no need to worry whether these houses would withstand the storm; they were built to last.

But there was one more thing to do before she made the cake and that was to write her journal. She always tried to scribble a little of her life before the day became too dark to write. There was even less light on the stairs but Jane knew the cottage inside out and found her way to the spare bedroom easily. Taking out her current journal from the sea chest, she closed the lid then sat firmly on top to write today's entry. Noticing the ink on her index finger, she pushed it in her mouth and sucked it hard. This was a childish habit she had never thrown aside and probably never would. Some of the ink had gone but not all of it. She would wash it off properly downstairs, Sitting on the old chest again, although she did it daily, reminded her of those wonderful times at Ecclesmachan with Rob. The excitement stayed with her, even now, and she knew deep in her heart that Rob loved her. That was important. Living together was not. She must finish now. There were more important things to do.

As she moved towards the staircase, she noticed the ink was still on her finger and she sucked it again. Then, seeing how dark the staircase had become, she switched on the electric light.

000

Outside the door, as they knocked, the gale swirled round and round Stephanie's skirts and Andrew had to hold on to his tweed cap to save it from flying along the line of cottages without him.

"I wonder why she doesn't come," he said, jumping up and down with the cold. I know, I'll go round to the back door and see if she's there. She must be in. It's so wild outside that she would hardly have decided to go shopping or visiting. I expect the radio's on."

It would be nice to have that cup of tea he had been talking about and Fiona needed to be indoors, out of this gale-force wind. So Andrew opened the back door, knowing it was never locked. It would have been most anti-social to have excluded Rob from entering Jane's cottage when he felt like it. Hmph!

He walked through the kitchen, sniffing the air. No cake smells then. That was unusual, when they were expected back for tea. It was a total of half a dozen steps before he reached the front door and the foot of the stairs.

Oh no! His mother was lying out, with her eyes wide open and it was simple to see that she was dead. He had no need to check for a pulse at wrist or throat. He had no need to listen for a breath. But she looked so neat. Not a bit like someone who had fallen down a full flight of stairs. What freak of nature had ensured that her skirts still covered her legs and her arms were only slightly apart. She looked as if she had been placed there.

"Stephanie! Steph! Come here quickly – round the back!" Andrew called frantically at the window.

The door was open and Andrew just stood there, his hand on his cheek, his eyes staring through the house as Stephanie came in. Then she looked towards the front door, down at the floor.

There, in front of them, was the supine body of Jane, dressed in her white, full-length apron. She was lying on her back, one leg bent and draped over the other and both arms by her sides. Stephanie also thought she looked as if she had been deliberately positioned this way for a photograph. She was smiling, as if pleased to see everybody but her normally gentle eyes were fixed, wide open, staring.

"She's dead. My mother's dead. What can I do?"

Stephanie had to take charge. "I'll get Rob," she said, grabbing the pushchair as she opened the door and ran round to the next little house. The knocker was in the shape of a sheep's head with horns at each side and it was painted green to match the door. What strange things people noticed when they were in a panic. The noise of her knocking reverberated in the room beyond.

"What on earth's the matter," Rob said, when he saw her standing wet and dishevelled on the step, Fiona in the pushchair behind her, looking extremely frightened and about to cry. "I was sharpening my secateurs…"

"Jane's dead. On the floor. Andrew's there with her. I don't know what to do. Help me, Rob!" She could feel her voice rising up and up with every syllable.

"I don't believe it!" Rob said the first thing that came into his head. Then he took another close look at Stephanie, clutching the handle of her drenched pushchair and she knew he believed her.

"Come here. Come in. There's a fire in the grate. Just put some more coal on it to get a blaze. Towels are in the drawer for you and the bairn. Make some tea. I must go and see…" his voice dwindled as he knew what he must do.

She watched him run out of the cottage and down the garden path and knew his mind must be in turmoil, wishing he had been there to save his love from this terrible end. The gate swung open and she heard it clanging, as he left it swinging open in the wind. Then Jane's gate did the same and he strode out of sight, around the house corner. If she lived til she was ninety, Stephanie knew the sound of a squeaking gate would bring back everything about that dreadful day.

She had a vision of Andrew's kneeling on the floor, as she left the house. He had been holding one of his mother's hands in his and rubbing it as if to bring back some life but his eyes stared into the middle distance as he worked away and it was obvious that he knew he could do nothing..

Stephanie never once thought she should go back there. The two men needed to be together, with the woman they had shared for so long. Her little girl sat silently in front of her, her wet curls escaping from her woollen hat and her eyes like saucers in her serious face. She had never once cried out, not even when she was left alone on her granny's doorstep. It was as if she knew that something dreadful had happened and did not want to cause more fuss to her tormented parents.

CHAPTER 47

The doctor was called and he certified death from electrical shock. It was discovered that Jane had had a weak heart and never told anyone, so the amount of electricity she received through her hand had been enough to kill her, whereas a younger, stronger person might well have survived to tell the tale. He had said it was strange that she got a shock but she must have touched the metal switch with wet hands.

After the precious body had been removed, all that was left to do was to tidy the kitchen of its multifarious contents. It was clear to anyone that Jane had been about to bake a cake before the dreadful accident had happened. Stephanie started to put away the ingredients in the larder, knowing exactly where everything went because she had watched Jane at work so often and had helped to clear up during their long conversations together.

When Andrew had come to Rob's to collect his wife and daughter, Stephanie knew that her initial thoughts about their being together at this dreadful time had been wrong.

"Why did you let him come in? I don't want him anywhere near me," Andrew had said on the gravel path, through his tears. It was no use going on about thinking it was the right thing to do, because she knew that everything she said would be ignored at that awful time, so she remained silent.

It was pointless trying to reason with him now, so the best place for the other grieving man was in his own home and that is where he went, walking like a ghost himself. What a lucky woman Jane had been, to have his love all through her adult life.

What would Rob do now?

CHAPTER 48

On the day of the funeral, Stephanie heard the doorbell ring and stopped drying the dishes, putting down her tea towel on the back of one of the old wooden chairs in the farm cottage kitchen. It was just a few steps to the front door but she stopped momentarily at the little mirror in the hallway to run her hands over the top of her hair and flick her thick plait to the front, before greeting the man in overalls standing patiently on the step. It was such an old-fashioned hairstyle for the seventies. She felt she really must have it cut. But her hair wasn't the only thing she wanted to tidy. She had been crying since the men left the house.The man nodded in her direction and said, "I thought nobody was in. I was just going to take this back to the depot. What a good thing you came to the door. I'll be glad to get this heavy old thing delivered today. Don't fancy coming all this way again on Friday."

She had no idea what on earth he was talking about. She hadn't ordered anything recently and anyway he said it was a heavy old thing.

"I'm sorry, I think you must have made a mistake. We're not expecting anything big and heavy – in fact we're not expecting anything at all."

"Oh no m'dear! Don't say they've got it wrong again. I'll kill those eejuts in the office. Let me check these papers though. Maybe it's for somebody ye ken. Now, let me see, Miss Fiona Donaldson, Farmtoun Cottage, Uphall, is that you?"

"No, I'm Mrs Donaldson, but it's my little daughter. Who could have sent her something by carrier. She's only a baby of two years old. Could you tell me what it is and I might have more of an idea? Someone must have got the name wrong. Maybe it was for me."

"Aye, lass, it's a bloody great box," the carrier continued. "Sorry, missus, I didn't mean to swear. I suppose some people call 'em chests, if you'll pardon the expression."

"Goodness! Whatever next? Who did it come from?"

"I canna help you there, hen. I just collect stuff, ye ken. I'm sorry lass. If you would just sign this bit o' paper, I'll offload your box and be on my way."

The box was made from old grained, heavily veined wood and it had a slightly convex lid which overhung the main part of it. There were scratches and indentations on the top and some peculiar 'L' shaped marks which looked as if they had been dug out with a penknife. Stephanie was loathe to touch it at first but once it was in the room it somehow looked at home and she could imagine dressing it up with a few bright cushions and using it as a window seat. They were a bit short of furniture. However, it was not hers and, no doubt, Andrew would have ideas of his own, even though it had been sent to their daughter, but by whom. It must be a mistake.

Fiona was their pride and joy and had been the joy of her poor, dead granny, Jane. Andrew was away at the funeral now, with his brother, Henry.

He had asked repeatedly if Jane would come and live with them. She had not been happy about that idea; wanted to stay in her own little cottage on the far side of the village, next door to Rob, her great friend.

Stephanie was disappointed that she seemed unable to have any more children. But she had been to the doctor last week and had a thorough check-up and he said there were a few problems but they were not insurmountable. Remembering the way she had felt when she had Fiona, she was sure she was pregnant again but it was early days and she knew she shouldn't try to self-diagnose. If the doctor said problems, there must be problems. She must be patient.

000

She decided to have a closer look at the old chest. She just supposed it fascinated her because she had no idea where it came from. It looked like an old sea chest. She felt she was being nosy and it actually belonged to somebody else. But something made her want to find out more about it. Nobody would know, would they?

She knelt down on the rag rug by the hearth to pull up the lid, noticing that there was a metal loop and eye but no padlock and once she had it open she understood why. The chest was completely empty. She peered at the inside of the lid which had been painted in a naïve fashion and depicted sea-waves all round the four sides; the centre was decorated with a crown bearing a cross on top and jewels around it. On either side of this were unrecognizable flags and then there were trees at each side of the flags, a deciduous and a conifer, something a sailor might long for during his long voyages. The conifers were repeated in the same muted colours of brown, red and ochre on compartments at each side of the main box, hinges of brass held on the lid and the same brass was used for strengthening, in the form of 'L' plates at each corner on the top surface. It was obviously very old.

She stood up to listen for any sounds, knowing she had been some time investigating the chest but all was quiet on the road outside and she could see through the two little, multi-paned windows if anyone arrived in a car, so she returned to her meticulous viewing. Fiona was asleep anyway and it would be a while before she awoke. She had no idea why she felt it should be such a secret but something inside her knew this was not just an ordinary sea chest and that there was a story about it that she had yet to discover. Little did she know that she was about to find out everything about her husband's mother and her amazing life.

Inside the chest, there were long, narrow compartments with lids at each side and Stephanie lifted the left-hand one to find a divided box, underneath which were two small drawers, also painted. It struck her that the sailor who had painted this had had plenty of time on his hands, probably on board ship and he had probably constructed it for himself whilst enjoying some time on dry land, in preparation for filling it with his clothing and personal possessions. It was sad to think that all men on board ship held the paraphernalia of their whole lives in a box the size of that which would carry them off at the end.

When she lifted the lid of the right-hand side compartment, the space beneath seemed shallow, compared with its partner and she wondered why this should be so. Curious by nature, she felt around the space and realised that there was a double thickness of wood. Putting a hand at either end she tugged upwards and was rewarded by movement. On her second try, the whole section came upwards and out of the box. Her energetic efforts had deposited her on the floor, still clutching the box from the interior. She placed it to one side, got onto her knees and peered into the space she had made.

Inside this dark, confined space were canvas bound books, most of them the same size. One or two smaller ones had been squeezed into the ends, hence there had been no rattling when the carrier had deposited the trunk earlier. She tentatively reached out to the topmost book and reverently stroked its spine. What were these hidden volumes and how had they arrived there?

Looking around her as if checking for watching intruders yet all the time knowing she was almost alone in the house, apart from Fiona, asleep in the next room, she pulled out the inch-thick maroon book. It was like starting a new exercise book at school; all the excitement of a new page was yet to be revealed but this time she hoped it would be full and not the pristine blank pages of schooldays. Inside the cover she read in beautiful Italic writing,

THIS IS THE JOURNAL OF JANE ELIZABETH DONALDSON, STARTED ONE WEEK AFTER HER MARRIAGE TO MICHAEL DONALDSON ON 10TH MARCH 1920. THESE NOTES WILL BE A SECRET UNTIL I DIE.

Oh! How dreadful! The chest was from Jane. So how had it come to Fiona, when her granny was dead? And she must have kept it well hidden because Stephanie had never seen it before. She had written those words as a young wife, never imagining in her wildest dreams that one day someone else would read her private thoughts. Stephanie almost put the book back, feeling like a sneaky criminal reading someone else's personal diary and then commonsense took over and she had to know more about this strong woman who had been her icon for so long. The volume lay open at the first page while she composed herself for turning to the start of the story.

Jane had met her husband Michael when she was eighteen
…

Stephanie continued to read the fascinating story of the woman she had loved for many years. The sound of birds in the tree outside the window interrupted Stephanie's concentration and she immediately returned to the present moment. She glanced down at her wrist watch and saw that it was two o'clock in the afternoon and she had been sitting on the floor for an hour. She was so involved in Jane's complicated journal that she fully expected to see Michael coming through the door. This was ridiculous.

She stood up, hearing her knees crack after spending so much time on the hard floor and rubbed her calves to disperse the pins and needles. Without thinking twice, she put the diary back where it had been and thrust the box shelf down on top of the collection of books. It wasn't so much a feeling of guilt but one of possessiveness; she wanted to know all there was to know, before anyone else. It was a long chance but she hoped against hope that Andrew would not have the curiosity to find the hidden compartment immediately. If he did, he did.

She advanced on the kitchen like Boadicea and threw pots and pans around until she had produced the beginnings of a nourishing meal for the wanderer's return. She was sure that he had taken only the minimum of sustenance during this sad day and she intended to restore his spirits as soon as he returned.

Just after half-past the hour, the key turned in the lock and a miserable person entered their happy home. She put her arms around her sad, beloved husband, hugging him close and then held her finger to her mouth, to intimate no necessity to speak at present. He smiled a thankful, melancholy smile and went off to remove his funereal clothing. There was no need for words – she knew how he must feel.

While he was gone, she heard Fiona crying in her cot, so went to lift her out.

Andrew came into the room at that moment and tipped his head in affection. Then, without hesitation, he strode towards his family and wrapped his arms around his child and her mother. His eyes were full of unshed tears for his precious mother and Stephanie could do nothing for him. He had taken on the mantle of the strong and would not cast it off until bedtime, when she hoped she could be of some comfort.

After their meal, Stephanie played on the floor with Fiona's wooden blocks and talked to her whilst doing so but she could feel Andrew's depression like a heavy cloak, covering them all as she attempted to take the weight off his shoulders.

Stephanie was glad Fiona was too young to know that her kind granny was never going to look after her again and she silently promised to tell her all about Jane when she was a little older.

CHAPTER 49

Since Margaret had become a doctor in Broxburn, Stephanie and Andrew had seen little of her and Henry, due to their busy lives, apart from today when Andrew's brother had collected him in his car, to take him to the funeral in Uphall. Stephanie kept wondering what had become of Rob. He just seemed to disappear into the woodwork after Jane died, poor man. No doubt he was at the funeral and she hoped the two brothers had made up their differences with him. There was no need to be at loggerheads at such a sad time and he needed some comfort.

. She was feeling introspective for another reason, anyway. She had been to the doctor's yesterday, firmly convinced that she was pregnant again and this time she believed there would be a happy outcome. Even so she had not told Andrew, although she had meant to all the time they were in Linlithgow. Anyway, she was too sad to be pleased now and even wondered whether she should tell Andrew at all, in the present circumstances. It seemed to be a habit of hers, to keep her childbearing to herself until she was absolutely sure. Jane would have understood.

However, she had had second thoughts and decided she would choose her moment and then cheer up her dear husband with this wonderful news. What better way to take his mind off his grief for a while?

When Andrew arrived home from the funeral, she could tell immediately that it not that special moment. He retired into himself and hardly had a word to say about the church proceedings, or the people present. Apart, that is, from one person.

"That bloody gardener was there again. What do you think of that?"

"I fully expected he would be. Andrew, why do you hate him so much now? I thought you used to like him a lot."

"I suppose it's because he didn't do what I wanted him to do. He should have taken the load off my mother, married her and made her acceptable, instead of which he turned her into laughing stock, someone with a good friend next door. No woman has a man for a friend these days!"

"Oh Andrew, I know you're overwrought but you mustn't talk like that. I'm sure they came to that conclusion between them. It can't have been one-sided."

"Henry feels the same. We could hardly bring ourselves to speak to him today. I hope he knows why."

"Well, I think you were very cruel. He must be suffering terribly. After all, he stuck with Jane for years and years. He could easily have gone off with someone else, and married them."

"Oh, to hell with him and everything else. I'm not in the mood to discuss relationships. I'm whacked. I'm going to bed. I'm sorry, Stephanie. It's been a bad day. Do you know, the lawyer came right up to me after the funeral and said he will be coming to read the will on Monday. Fancy my mother even making a will – she didn't have that much to leave anybody."

"Oh, I forgot to tell you, one of her items has arrived already. I'm sure you remember it, an old sea chest. Jane's left it to Fiona. It's over there by the wall. I thought you would have noticed."

"I'm not in the mood for noticing anything, let alone that old bit of wood she used to keep in the garden shed. My father couldn't stand the sight of it. He banished it to an outhouse. Huh," he shrugged and took himself off to bed.

Her news would have to wait until she had an interested audience and that wasn't to be for a few days.

000

Rob turned up after the weekend, to hear the will read. Andrew was collecting his newspaper and Henry had not arrived, when Rob came to the door.

"Oh Rob. I'm so glad to see you," Stephanie said, meaning every word. He was a kind and thoughtful man and had always treated her well, asking questions about her past and present interests and telling her many of his own inner thoughts when they were left alone. She felt he needed a female ear, now his life-long friend had gone.

"I'm glad to see you as well, Stephanie," he said and she could see him looking over her shoulder into the room, as he turned down the collar of his mackintosh.

"Andrew is at the newsagents. It's just the two of us for a while," she said, standing back so he could enter.

"I can't pretend I'm not glad. Those two boys of Jane's did everything but throw me out of the church at the funeral service. I had made up my mind to keep a low profile but they weren't content with that. They barged in front of me and showed me to a pew right at the back. I couldn't believe they were the same two I used to ferry around in my van and the lads I taught how to wield a spade and fork. It was unbelievable. But perhaps you can tell me why it's happened. Was it something I did?"

"No, Rob. I'm afraid it's something you didn't do," she said, as she took his coat and hung it up in the hall. "I have to be honest with you, they felt you should have married their mother and now ... now it's too late ... but I don't have to tell you that."

"Stephanie, you're a lot like your mother-in-law, the way you come straight out with things and don't beat about the bush. I know I can't explain to Andrew and Henry but I feel I can tell you a little about my relationship with Jane. For a while I couldn't take on the commitment of marriage and I told her my life story and how my own father ruined his marriage. Then I asked Jane to marry me and she turned me down. I have to admit I was glad she did at that time and we discussed the whole thing, in detail. She said there had been a time when she would happily have accepted my proposal but that she had come to the conclusion that we were better the way we were.

"In other words, the situation we had suited us both and we left it at that. I have to say I'm glad it never came to anything official. That way it remains a dream. If we'd married, it would have been like waiting for the newness to wear off, just like buying a new car and waiting for the first patch of rust."

"Rob, I think I understand but I don't think anybody else would. What do you want me to tell Andrew?"

"Just say we made up our minds not to marry and, because we were never going to have children, we felt it didn't really matter."

"Alright," she said, just in time, because the door opened and in walked Andrew, followed by Henry.

"Oh, hello Rob," he said, curtly. "I've just seen the lawyer. He's parking his car and will be here shortly. I suggest we sit round the table and he can go through his papers."

The whole morning felt formal and almost as if none of them knew the others. There was that air of expectancy, tinged with sadness and it all felt terribly unreal. After the first legal blurb about Last Will and Testament, the lawyer seemed to relax and all eyes were on him, to find out the mystery of Jane's bequests. The first part was about her house, which was to be shared by Andrew and Henry.

Stephanie was left her kitchen contents, Fiona the sea chest and Margaret her books.

"Mrs Donaldson also held money in a bank account, which my legal firm was informed were the proceeds from paintings and furniture once owned by a Mrs Grace Sanderson and which were sold at the time of her divorce from Mr Michael Donaldson. This money has accrued over the years and you can see the figures, as I pass them round."

They all stared at the piece of typed paper and made various noises of amazement, as they saw in black and white what Jane had actually had tucked under her metaphorical mattress. Then came the shock.

"This money goes to her loyal friend and companion, Robert Barclay, with thanks and fondest wishes, with no suggestions as to how he will use it, because, as she wrote, 'It will be the right way'.

"That is all I have to say. Please feel free to ask me questions about the document I have just quoted."

There was absolute silence in the room and then Andrew turned to his brother and opened his mouth to speak. Stephanie could see by the expression on his face that his comment was not going to be pleasant but before he could say one word, Rob stood up at the end of the table, where he had been lounging, albeit miserably, during the whole session.

"Could I speak to you all, particularly while Mr McLeod is present because I want this to be a legally binding statement. Jane Donaldson was my friend and companion, as she says I was hers. I did not know anything about her money, nor do I wish to accept it. I would like it to be shared between her two sons, as is their right, and I would be pleased if this could be written down by you, Mr McLeod and added to the document which sits in front of you."

Once again, not a word was said. Stephanie put her hand on top of Andrew's, partly to comfort him and partly to stop him from making a fool of himself. She had sensed that he was about to throw himself into a tirade about Rob and all she wanted was to discourage him from insulting this fine person. Who else in the world did he know who would pass on a not-insubstantial inheritance within minutes, or indeed seconds, of receiving it. No deep thought process had been involved, before Rob handed over a sum of money which would have kept him in comfort for the remaining days of his life. But he was a man who didn't need money; all he cared about was nature, so he had done what was right. Jane would have been proud of him.

She felt Andrew's hand turn over until their fingers were clasped together and, when she looked, his face was looking gently, calmly at hers. Then he transferred the same expression to Rob and said one sentence,

"Rob, I don't deserve this."

Henry thrust his hand over the table to take Rob's and said, "Neither do I."

Rob just sat there, smiling enigmatically at the two of them, then he stood and carefully pushed back his chair, signalled goodbye to the lawyer and left, hitching his raincoat off the hook as he went. He would be happy that Jane's sons had made up with him, even though it took money to do it.

As he walked to the door, he said, "By the way, I hope Fiona got the sea chest. Jane said I should send it to the bairn if anything happened to her." His eyes were starting to fill with tears, so he opened the door and left.

The busy little lawyer started shuffling his papers around, then took a pen from his inside pocket and made some notes on a sheet of paper. All this time the rest of them were as if cast in stone. Nobody knew what to say. Mr McLeod stood up and

Stephanie walked ahead of him to the door, where she handed him his coat and hat.

"I will see that my final instruction is put in order, Mrs Donaldson and will be in contact soon," he said, once more the formal lawyer, and then he too left. As the door closed behind him, there was a communal sigh from the brothers, as they drifted over to more comfortable armchairs near the fire and started to talk. Stephanie had never heard her husband speaking so quietly.

But she simply had to interrupt their calm scene. "As this is the time for surprises and formal speeches, do you all mind if I also make one," she said, looking conspiratorially at Margaret.

"I have known for several months that I'm going to have another child", she said. "And the doctor has confirmed it."

As the rush of congratulations rained down and the hugs and kisses surrounded her in warmth, she thought of Jane. She would have been so pleased, so happy to know that her son was going to be a father again.

THE END

www.ingramcontent.com/pod-product-compliance
Lightning Source LLC
Chambersburg PA
CBHW052210090526
44584CB00016BA/1894